This book is applicable for every school leader. *What Can I Take Off Your Plate?* is also a valuable resource in principal preparation programs for future leaders. It guides leaders to better understand the importance of an integrated systems approach and provides numerous practical ideas for ways to support the most valuable asset in a school—the teachers.

—Dr. Todd Whitaker
research professor, University of Missouri; author of 65 books

As a former principal, this is the book I wish existed my first few years in the job. WOW! The ability to filter, prioritize, and support a staff of educators is paramount and one of the most challenging aspects of leadership. Jill and Lara do a phenomenal job integrating stories, ideas, working documents, resources, and so much more in *What Can I Take Off Your Plate?* HIGHLY recommended!

—Adam Welcome
keynote speaker, author, podcast host, former principal

Combating burnout and solving the current teacher retention problem constitutes one of the most significant challenges facing us in education today. In *What Can I Take Off Your Plate?*, Jill Handley and Lara Donnelly have created a masterful and comprehensive solution that recognizes the need for true systemic change. By powerfully addressing root causes and providing structural shifts and strategies that go far beyond quick fixes, they have written a book that will surely move the needle and positively influence any school culture.

—Dave Burgess
author of *Teach Like a Pirate*; president, Dave Burgess Consulting, Inc.

What Can
I Take Off
Your
Plate?

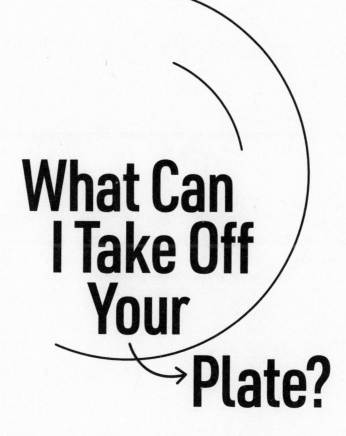

ASCD MEMBER BOOK

Many ASCD members received this book as a
member benefit upon its initial release.

Learn more at: **www.ascd.org/memberbooks**

JILL **HANDLEY**
LARA **DONNELLY**

What Can I Take Off Your Plate?

A Structural—and Sustainable—Approach to Countering Teacher Burnout

ascd

Arlington, Virginia USA

2800 Shirlington Rd., Suite 1001 • Arlington, VA 22206 USA
Phone: 800-933-2723 or 703-578-9600 • Fax: 703-575-5400
Website: www.ascd.org • Email: member@ascd.org
Author guidelines: www.ascd.org/write

Richard Culatta, *Chief Executive Director;* Anthony Rebora, *Chief Content Officer;* Genny Ostertag, *Managing Director, Book Acquisitions and Editing;* Stephanie Bize, *Acquisitions Editor;* Mary Beth Nielsen, *Director, Book Editing;* Jamie Greene, *Senior Editor;* Georgia Park, *Senior Graphic Designer;* Valerie Younkin, *Senior Production Designer;* Kelly Marshall, *Production Manager;* Christopher Logan, *Senior Production Specialist;* Kathryn Oliver, *Creative Project Manager;* Shajuan Martin, *E-Publishing Specialist*

All web links in this book are correct as of the publication date below but may have become inactive or otherwise modified since that time. If you notice a deactivated or changed link, please email books@ascd.org with the words "Link Update" in the subject line. In your message, please specify the web link, the book title, and the page number on which the link appears.

PAPERBACK ISBN: 978-1-4166-3300-6   ASCD product #125002

PDF EBOOK ISBN: 978-1-4166-3301-3; see Books in Print for other formats.

Quantity discounts are available: email programteam@ascd.org or call 800-933-2723, ext. 5773, or 703-575-5773. For desk copies, go to www.ascd.org/deskcopy.

ASCD Member Book No. FY24-6 (August 2024 P). ASCD Member Books mail to Premium (P), Select (S), and Institutional Plus (I+) members on this schedule: Jan, PSI+; Feb, P; Apr, PSI+; May, P; Jul, PSI+; Aug, P; Sep, PSI+; Nov, PSI+; Dec, P. For current details on membership, see www.ascd.org/membership.

Library of Congress Cataloging-in-Publication Data
Names: Handley, Jill, author. | Donnelly, Lara, author.
Title: What can I take off your plate? : a structural-and sustainable-approach to countering teacher burnout / Jill Handley & Lara Donnelly.
Description: Arlington, Virginia : ASCD, [2024] | Includes bibliographical references and index.
Identifiers: LCCN 2024013263 (print) | LCCN 2024013264 (ebook) | ISBN 9781416633006 (paperback) | ISBN 9781416633013 (pdf)
Subjects: LCSH: Teachers—Job stress—Prevention. | Burn out (Psychology)—Prevention. | Teacher-administrator relationships.
Classification: LCC LB2840.2 .H25 2024 (print) | LCC LB2840.2 (ebook) | DDC 371.102—dc23/eng/20240429
LC record available at https://lccn.loc.gov/2024013263
LC ebook record available at https://lccn.loc.gov/2024013264

30 29 28 27 26 25 24   1 2 3 4 5 6 7 8 9 10 11 12

*This book is dedicated to my daughters Sydney and Madison,
my two reasons for everything I do.—Jill*

*This book is dedicated to my daughter, Mary Katherine,
who has inspired me to be a better educator and human.
This is for you, sweet girl.—Lara*

WHAT CAN I TAKE OFF YOUR PLATE?

Introduction

Teacher burnout … have you heard about it? Who are we kidding? If you're breathing and an educator, you've no doubt heard the term countless times. Nevertheless, even though you know the term, do you know what it really means and its true impact? According to Maslach and Leiter (2016), burnout is the emotional response to workplace stress over time. Its impact before the COVID-19 pandemic was startling:

- Approximately 15 percent of teachers in the United States resign every year (Rankin, 2016).
- The number of teachers who resign in the first five years is about 41 percent (Rankin, 2016).
- About 66 percent of highly ranked teachers in the United States leave for another profession (Rankin, 2016).
- Approximately $7 billion is spent in the United States every year due to the impact of teacher turnover (Luhombo et al., 2023).

Teacher burnout is not a new phenomenon by any stretch of the imagination. It is an idea that has been researched since the 1960s and continues to plague the educational profession. What is it about teacher burnout that continues to dominate the narrative in education?

Research shows that emotional labor and emotional exhaustion have a significant impact on teacher burnout. In addition, Yao and colleagues (2015) examined the antecedent that most influences emotional labor and determined it to be school climate. The authors broke school climate into collaboration, student relations, decision making, school resources, and instructional innovation. Understanding that school climate plays such an important role in the burnout of teachers, this book focuses heavily on ways you can support your staff to reduce the impact of burnout.

An abundance of research conducted prior to the COVID-19 pandemic focused on emotional labor and exhaustion (e.g., Bodenheimer, 2018; Keller et al., 2014; Richardson et al., 2008; Yao et al., 2015; Yin, 2011). Most of these researchers studied how surface acting and deep acting affect teachers' emotional labor. According to Yao and colleagues (2015), surface acting is when someone uses "fake emotions" in interactions to display the emotions that are expected in the situation. An example of this would be when a teacher meets with a disgruntled parent and the teacher pretends to be happy to meet with the parent or happy to work with their child. Deep acting, by contrast, is when someone genuinely tries to feel the emotions appropriate for a situation—such as empathy for a struggling student—that they might actually feel triggered by.

In addition to emotional labor and exhaustion, Garcia and Weiss (2019) report stark differences in staff beliefs between high- and low-poverty schools. The most significant differences were found in the level of safety, parental support, and administrator support and encouragement. Teachers who work in high-poverty schools report more student misbehavior, verbal threats, and physical attacks by students. Compare this with educators in low-poverty schools who report much higher support from parents. Garcia and Weiss broke down the data to describe why teachers were feeling the effects of burnout and considering leaving the profession into four main categories:

- Barriers to teaching
- Stress and physical safety
- Lack of administrative support
- Low satisfaction, motivation, and expectations

Since the pandemic began, the effects of burnout have been even more significant. The additional responsibilities teachers assume have intensified, creating increased stress and job dissatisfaction. In addition, staff shortages increase teachers' workloads and require them to do more with less, leaving them to feel overworked, under-resourced, and unappreciated. Although many schools and districts have made an effort to encourage self-care in the workplace, teachers are tired of hearing how changing their mindset will mitigate their compassion fatigue. If schools are going to combat high rates of teacher attrition in these challenging times, leaders must take a systemic approach and focus their time, efforts, and resources on the things they can control. To make meaningful and sustainable change that will retain teachers and alleviate the compounded effects of teacher burnout, leaders must reduce the challenges teachers face by actively taking things off their collective plate.

Even though a heartbreaking 15 percent of teachers were leaving the profession every year prior to the pandemic, that statistic more than doubled by 2022 when one in three teachers reported that they were considering leaving the profession (Rankin, 2022), and that was a conservative finding! The National Education Association reported that more than *half* of their teachers planned to quit or retire early because of burnout (Sparks, 2022). To say that the impact of burnout is a critical issue is an understatement; it's a crisis.

With this in mind, there is one essential question administrators should be asking every teacher: *What can we take off your plate?*

Until now, most books on this topic have provided strategies for ways teachers can combat the burnout themselves. Although providing self-care strategies will provide teachers with resources to better

> *They should be asking educators, "What is the most time-consuming part of your job? What tasks aren't as important? What are the systems we can put in place so you can do the work that you think matters most?"*
>
> —Tim Walker

balance their emotional well-being, if we truly want to combat teacher burnout, then we must evaluate the current systems and structures in our schools and take steps to reduce teachers' frustration and sense of feeling overwhelmed. Instead of asking teachers to fix their own burnout, leaders must create and cultivate an environment that attracts and retains teachers for the long haul. Integral to that is a focus on what we *can* control. "When people come to work with a higher sense of purpose, they find it easier to weather hard times or even find opportunity in those hard times" (Sinek, 2009, p. 101).

It is necessary to triage the most pressing factors, but to truly combat teacher burnout, school leaders must develop systems and structures that not only provide short-term relief but also develop a culture of long-term sustainability. When everything seems to be burning down around us, we know it's hard to think about doing anything except extinguishing the emergency fires. However, we can't wait for things to "get better" before starting work on long-term sustainability. If we want teachers to take better care of their students, then we must take better care of our teachers.

In this book, you will find strategies and resources for both short-term triage and long-term sustainability. If we are going to win the war against teacher burnout, then we need a combination of both. This book is therefore divided into three sections that are intentionally designed to reduce burnout and tackle the reasons teachers are leaving the profession in record numbers.

Part I includes three major components that affect teacher motivation and satisfaction: alignment of purpose woven throughout meaningful systems, the gift of time by intentional collaboration, and effective communication. Part II focuses on supporting the whole teacher by removing barriers to teaching, increasing physical safety, decreasing stress, and increasing overall support. The chapters in this section include behavior support inside the classroom, coaching and feedback, and promoting a work-life balance. Part III addresses ways to triage burnout and stop the bleeding now, so feel free to skip to this section for more immediate action solutions. We acknowledge that these chapters do not provide a long-term fix, but they can help provide some immediate relief by tapping into appreciation, fun, and sustainability—and by combating teacher shortages.

Most teachers entered the profession to make a difference and have a positive impact on the future of the students they serve each day. Therefore, they deserve to wake up, go to work, and not have their passion slowly (or quickly) extinguished by the factors that lead to burnout. As leaders, we are in a unique position to create environments that inspire others to take part in—and remain in—a system that changes lives every single day.

Jill Handley, EdD, is the assistant superintendent of multilingual learners for one of the largest urban districts in the United States. Previously, Jill was the proud principal of an elementary school for 16 years. Lara Donnelly, EdD, had the opportunity to work and collaborate with Jill for 13 of those years as the professional school counselor. Together, we achieved numerous recognitions for our school, including National School of Character, National Distinguished ESEA school, and the first Family Friendly school in the state of Kentucky.

Despite all the recognition, we are most proud of the culture and climate we built to ensure the success of both students and staff. That culture and climate led to a very high teacher satisfaction and retention rate, and there were several years where we maintained 100 percent teacher retention. Most of the teachers who did choose to leave either retired or moved schools within the district (often to be closer to their home and family). Due to the success of the overall culture and climate, we have presented and shared this work at multiple national conferences.

We know that some of you are likely thinking, "That all sounds great, but what are the demographics of your school?" This is a valid question. Our school has just shy of 600 students, of which about 85 percent qualify for free or reduced-price lunch and 44 percent are multilingual learners receiving English language development (ELD) services, and there are more than 30 languages represented.

After years of watching educators walk through our building and hearing them comment on our culture and how good our building "feels"—and asking us both how we created that feeling and how we retain the teachers we have—we finally decided it was time to share the research-based, tried-and-true strategies that work if you are consistent in your implementation. Our goal is not simply to share theory with you; we also want to share a systems and structures approach that helps streamline everything you do as an administrator and leader.

This book is for every school leader who has felt exhausted from spinning their wheels and constantly putting out fires. It is for school leaders who regularly feel like they are taking five steps backward for every two steps forward. It is for leaders who, regardless of their experience, struggle to find a work-life balance and often feel like they give more to their school family than they do to the one at home. This book is also for the leaders who have lost the passion for what they do—and are experiencing their own burnout. Finally, in this post-pandemic world, this book is for all of us: the school leaders who are barely keeping their heads above water and looking for a life vest to save their teachers, their school, and themselves.

PART I

Systems and Structures
That Combat Low
Teacher Motivation
and Satisfaction

1

Purpose Through Alignment

*"Vision without action is merely a dream. Action without vision
just passes the time. Vision with action can change the world."*

—Joel A. Barker

> **▭▭▯ Burnout Challenge**
>
> To support the diverse needs of students, teachers are often asked to
> try new initiatives and curriculum materials, many of which fade away
> within a couple of years. This cycle of "the next great thing" creates
> frustration and a lack of investment for teachers. In addition, when
> districts and schools say yes to too many initiatives, it creates com-
> peting priorities for teachers, making it difficult to build long-term
> capacity.

Mrs. Osko left the teachers' lounge feeling overwhelmed by a conversation
she just had with two colleagues about a new reading curriculum their
school would be adopting the following year. Even though the reading
scores at her elementary school indicated that something different needed
to be done in the area of literacy, she just wasn't sure this was the right time.
If adopted, the new reading curriculum would require more than 30 hours
of professional development—on top of the professional development

already scheduled for the school's initiatives to support trauma-informed care, personalized learning, and standards-based grading.

As a third-year teacher, Mrs. Osko already felt pulled in 100 different directions, trying to get better at everything the school already had going on. As she walked back to her classroom, her teammate's words kept running through her head: "Don't worry—I'm sure this initiative won't be around long. It's only a matter of time before the next great thing comes along." Ultimately, Mrs. Osko just wanted to do what was best for her students, but trying to navigate all the new initiatives simultaneously didn't make it easy.

Sound familiar? A few of the many challenges we face as leaders involve helping staff stay on track and focused on the destination (and see how all the pieces fit together) when external factors attempt to derail us. Without a clearly defined direction, we are certain to get lost along the way, and a lack of leadership clarity can lead to confusion and frustration for everyone involved.

To support the diverse needs of students, teachers are often asked to try new initiatives and curriculum materials, many of which inevitably fade away within a few years. The cycle created by constantly looking for "the next great thing" results in frustration and a lack of investment. In addition, when districts and schools take on too many initiatives, it adds additional requirements to an already full plate and creates competing priorities for teachers, thus making it difficult to build long-term capacity.

In *The Lighthouse Effect*, Steve Pemberton (2021) discusses the importance of establishing a North Star to guide you toward your mission and goals. As leaders responsible for so many things, it is easy to become immersed in the day-to-day operations of the work, feeling as though we spend more time reactively putting out fires than we do proactively supporting our goals. With so many competing priorities at the local and district levels, understanding how best to prioritize the work can become overwhelming, and many leaders are uncertain where to begin. The problem is that if we as leaders fail to establish priorities, that lack of focus and vision will undoubtedly trickle down to our staff and affect overall teacher satisfaction and motivation.

Teachers routinely identify their workload and increased demands of the profession as one of the primary reasons they choose to leave the profession (Betz, 2023). As we determine what we can take off their plates, it's essential to know which things align with the school's goal. However, before we can determine that, we must first establish goals that are grounded in a shared mission and vision: the *real* one—not just the one that hangs in the front lobby.

The first long-term foundational element for reducing teacher burnout is establishing a collective shared vision that unites staff around common goals and guides all your decision making. We've found (both in our own work and in working with others) that when a school hasn't engaged in the work of establishing a collective shared vision and committed to the action steps they will take to achieve that vision, there is an absence of or a breakdown in cohesive systems that align the day-to-day work in which teachers and leaders engage. This leaves everyone feeling as though they are juggling initiatives in silos and trying not to let anything drop. The ideas presented in this chapter, therefore, both help leaders understand the steps they can take to relieve teachers from the pressure of trying "one more thing" and rationalize and clarify the importance of establishing systems and structures that are grounded in a collective shared vision.

Establishing and Revisiting Your Why

In *Start with Why,* Simon Sinek (2009) discusses the importance of starting with *why* and provides several examples of organizations and initiatives that failed because they started with the *what* or *how* instead. Think about a leader you admire, then think about what it was that attracted you to them in the first place. Odds are their words and actions inspired you because you had a shared belief around a common goal. They knew *why* they were engaged in a specific effort, and you understood and could relate to that. Now think about a leader for whom you had less admiration.

Was their *why* clear, or were they more focused on the *what* and *how* of the job? In brief, they knew *what* they were doing and *how* to get the job done, but they weren't clear on *why* they should be doing it. Although these are critical elements of a successful organization, it is the *why* that unites and inspires us.

To explain why we do what we do, Sinek (2009) proposes an alternative perspective to existing assumptions about how successful leaders inspire, innovate, and achieve in a concept he calls the Golden Circle. The Golden Circle consists of three concentric circles that include the *why, how,* and *what. Why* is at the center and acts as a reminder that when we start by examining our purpose and work outward, it can positively influence our culture and have profound and long-lasting results.

As educators, our *why* is the reason we entered education in the first place. It is what motivates us to send glitter-filled envelopes in welcome back letters and what keeps us going even on our most challenging days. The truth is, our *why* is often easy to remember on our first day back—when everyone feels rested and rejuvenated after summer break—but our grasp of it tends to slip away by October . . . and is almost nonexistent by March.

Sometimes cynics and critics try to downplay the importance of establishing and revisiting the *why* and insist that the focus should be on the *what.* It's true that knowing your *what* provides guidance, but staying grounded in your *why* will keep you inspired, which is why we must revisit it often. Sinek posits, "When a *why* goes fuzzy, it becomes more difficult to maintain the growth, loyalty, and inspiration that helped drive the original success" (2009, p. 50).

We can tell you from personal experience that we have revisited our *why* with our staff multiple times in different ways, and we always leave with a rejuvenated passion and purpose for *what* we do. Whether you are visiting your *why* for the first time or revisiting it with your staff for the 25th time, we think you will find the ideas presented in Figure 1.1 meaningful to use as a beginning-of-the-year or a midyear revitalization activity.

FIGURE 1.1	
Steps to Lead Your Staff Through Revisiting Their *Why*	
Step 1	As a leader, share a personal story about your *why*.
Step 2	Ask staff to reflect on their *why* and share it with a colleague.
Step 3	As a fun, community-building activity, have staff members create a graphic representation of their *why* and hang it in their classrooms.
Step 4	Revisit your *why* often at staff meetings throughout the year so it becomes embedded in your mindset and practice.

For additional ideas about ways to find your *why* as an individual or as a team, check out *Find Your Why* (Sinek et al., 2017).

Identifying Core Values

Many of the ideas threaded throughout this chapter likely constitute work in which you have engaged at some point along your journey as a leader. Indeed, most is embedded in the work of graduate educational courses. Identifying core values, however, is not as commonly integrated. Nevertheless, determining core values according to your school's vision, mission, and culture and climate expectations helps tighten up all the other components. It also provides an anchor for all staff when making decisions with students, families, and one another.

Identifying core values is a critical component for the work in which leaders engage with their teams. In *Dare to Lead*, Brené Brown (2018) gives the following definition: "A value is a way of being or believing that we hold most important" (p. 186). Brown emphasizes that values are not simply something we determine but a daily practice. They are evident in our behaviors and the way we show up with our intentions and with others.

Determining what core values are most meaningful in your school should begin with your administrative team. Start with a list of generic core values (a quick Google search will get you everything you need), then choose which are most significant to help create the best possible culture and climate in your school. After the administrative team has determined two or three core values, have groups of teachers (such as the instructional leadership team or the equity committee) determine which they think would create the best possible climate and culture. Then have these teams return to their respective grade-level teams for input. By this point, most staff should have had some level of input. From here, the teams and committees responsible for gathering input can determine relevance and overlap of values and work with the administrative team to decide which values are most important to all staff.

Asking teacher leaders to discuss and bring feedback from their teams allows teachers and other staff members to discuss their thinking without the pressure of administration being present, making authentic conversations more likely. Consequently, core beliefs should be easier to determine among all staff, which in turn allows administration to take a pulse of teacher thinking—rather than just assume they have a good grasp on the collective opinion—and make decisions about how to communicate and implement the core values.

Other considerations include what to do when the core values of staff don't align with the core values of the school—and how to ensure you are hiring the candidate whose core values best align with your school. Many times, a misalignment of values between individuals and organizations creates stress, which could lead to burnout. It's important to note, however, that a misalignment of values doesn't necessarily indicate malintent or poor performance from either side. Nevertheless, teacher burnout has led to an increase in vacancies and a decline in education majors, which further erodes the teacher candidate pool. This situation has led many school leaders to be less discerning than they may want to be when considering applicants.

It is critical to have staff members whose core values align with your school's values, so we strongly caution against settling. Hiring to fill a vacancy without consideration for values alignment may be a short-term solution, but it could generate more long-term work as you create and cultivate a strong, sustainable culture grounded in your core values.

When we conduct interviews, the final question we ask each candidate is "What three words would others who know you use to describe you?" Invariably, this question provides more insight than any other. It has become clear that you can teach programs and skills, but you can't teach passion or alignment of values.

Creating a Shared Mission and Vision That Guide Your Work

If your leadership preparation was anything like mine (Jill), then there is a good chance an assignment in one of your classes, if not multiple classes, was to develop a mission statement for the school you would eventually lead. At the time, I didn't understand the true importance of this assignment; I saw it as another example of "busywork" on the road to principal certification. As such, I gave the assignment minimal effort. In fact, I still remember the key words I used in my internet search: *mission statement for elementary schools*. This search produced hundreds of examples, many of which included key phrases such as *academic excellence*, *high expectations*, and *educating all students at high levels*. By now, I'm sure you know what my next steps were. After reading through what seemed like hundreds of examples, I extracted the best buzzwords to wordsmith a mission statement for a school I would someday lead. I received an *A* on the assignment but didn't think about a mission statement again until I accepted my first job as a principal.

As a new principal, there were many things about which I was uncertain, but one thing I *knew* I had to do was craft a mission statement for my new school. Within the first few months, I revisited the mission statement I wrote for class. Knowing that I needed to get feedback from others, I sent my draft out in an email to staff and asked for suggestions. I got some feedback for a few cursory word revisions from one teacher, but most of what I received was some rendition of "sounds good"—or no response at all.

Nevertheless, I had done what I thought I needed to do to involve others, so my draft became our new mission and vision statement. We even had banners made for the building. I was so proud of myself for having completed one of the new principal "must-dos."

Fast-forward several years. Our district was undergoing major structural changes, including a new assistant superintendent. Prior to our first whole-group principal's meeting, our new leader asked each school to bring their mission and vision statements. As you can imagine, I was beaming with pride as I walked into the meeting. Not only did I have our statement to share, but I had a small version of the graphically designed banner that hung in our lobby. What happened next was a pivotal moment in my understanding of the difference between the wall decorations that hang in many organizations and the guiding principles great leaders use to unite their organization through a shared vision.

After each principal shared their school's mission statement, the assistant superintendent said it was clear we all still had work to do. I'll admit, I was a little put off at first, thinking about the time we would be wasting on something I had already done years ago. However, as the day progressed, our new boss provided the rationale and practical purpose for embracing a mission and vision statement. In addition, he provided examples of how his school's mission and vision guided leadership decisions, which led to improved school culture and increased achievement. By the end of the day, he had effectively debunked the myth of the meaningless mission statement and laid the foundational essentials in which all leaders should engage if they want people to follow them.

Prior to that day, the words *mission* and *vision* were used synonymously in our building. Schools must, however, understand the difference between the two before collaboratively developing them both. The mission and vision are the *what* of an organization: the outer circle ring of the Golden Circle.

Mission: What you do and who you are as an organization (i.e., establish the core value of why you exist)

Vision: What the organization wants to become (i.e., define its future self)

A mission statement should help ground your school in the shared values and beliefs that identify your purpose as an organization (Skrabanek, 2022). Schools without a collaboratively developed mission statement can have a lack of clarity, miscommunication, frustration, and disconnected staff members. Questions to guide the development of an effective mission statement include

- What do we do?
- Whom do we serve?
- How do we serve them?

By contrast, a vision statement should provide direction for your school and guide you toward established goals (Skrabanek, 2022). Schools without a collaboratively developed vision statement can have confusion about competing priorities and unmotivated and uninspired staff members. Questions to guide the development of an effective vision statement include

- What are our hopes and dreams?
- What problem are we solving for the greater good?
- Who and what are we inspiring to change?

The key to creating shared mission and vision statements is making sure you engage *all* stakeholders and include their collective voice. Although you may be the captain of the ship, failure to engage others will inevitably lead to crew members rowing in a variety of directions at once, which will result in a lack of movement or, even worse, leave you spinning in a circle of frustration.

After I got a better understanding of the purpose behind mission and vision statements, it became apparent that developing a shared mission and vision with staff must be a priority. In my welcome back letter to staff, I discussed the importance of working together to realign our priorities and goals as a school. Note that I did not use the words *mission* and *vision* at that time.

On our first staff day of that school year, staff members were divided into vertical teams and asked in advance to bring a photo of a child who meant a lot to them. The community building prompt for the morning was to share the photo and explain why the child was special. Within their vertical groups, staff members were then prompted to discuss what a "perfect school" would look like for the children in their photographs. After groups had time to brainstorm this open-ended question, they were given chart paper with one of five prompts:

- Describe the school we are trying to create.
- What would our school look like if it were a great place for students?
- What would our school look like if it were a great place for staff?
- It is five years from now and we have achieved our vision as a school. In what ways are we different?
- What assurances are we prepared to make to *every* student in our school?

Groups were given 10 minutes to discuss and address their prompts, making notes on the chart paper. They then rotated to the next station and prompt where they read the notes and thoughts written by the previous group. They then added to it. (Each group was given a different-colored marker to help differentiate their contributions.) This process continued until each group addressed all five prompts.

Next, the responses were typed up and shared with staff to provide an opportunity for additional feedback. Once the additional feedback was gathered, responses were analyzed to determine themes, which were then used to draft shared mission and vision statements. The drafts were shared with the staff for a final round of revisions. Finally, the instructional leadership team made recommendations to our site-based council to officially adopt the mission and vision statements.

Mission Statement: To educate the whole child and prepare each student to be a resilient learner and a globally and culturally competent citizen

Vision Statement: Kenwood Elementary is a caring and safe environment that strives to educate the whole child while promoting good character, responsibility, and academic success in every student. Kenwood students will maintain integrity, communicate effectively, and be critical thinkers/problem solvers. Kenwood will be among the most desired schools in Kentucky by students, parents, and employees.

The work does not stop once your staff has been through the process of creating the mission and vision statements. The purpose here is not to have a memento of something you can hang on the wall for the next 20 years; rather, the goal is to create a living, breathing guide that helps unite and inform decision making for your building. Your mission and vision statements should be updated as you make growth as a school. In fact, we recently went through the process of adopting new statements after only five years because our schoolwide goals had changed and grown. Part of our vision was to become one of the most desired schools in the state of Kentucky by students, parents, and employees—and after five years, we reached that goal! By letting our collective mission and vision drive our decision making, our school was recognized as a

- State and National School of Character
- Success Story School (Solution Tree)
- Bright Spot School (Prichard Committee)
- National ESEA Distinguished School
- Family Friendly School (first school in Kentucky to earn that certification)

As with core values, it is important to hire candidates whose personal and professional beliefs align with your school's mission and vision. Here is an idea Samantha Hamilton, principal of Goodman Elementary in Neosho, Missouri, shared on an episode of the *Be the Leader You Deserve* podcast

(Handley, 2022): "Create a video that includes elements from each teacher team demonstrating the school's mission and vision. Share the video with potential candidates and ask them to create a video that demonstrates how they can add value to achieving your school's mission and vision."

Making a Collective Commitment to Your Shared Mission and Vision

The day I met with our new assistant superintendent, I walked away with an understanding of the difference between *mission* and *vision*. I also walked away with the understanding that neither of those statements mattered without a collective commitment from staff to achieve them.

Collective commitments are what make the mission and vision a reality. They are assurances your staff makes in order to achieve the goals you set for yourselves as a school. In other words, they are the *how* of the Golden Circle. They can be approached and phrased in a variety of ways, but we chose to frame them using these sentence frames:

We believe _____. We commit to _____.

Collective commitments should be grounded in your core values—your *why*. They should outline your beliefs and what actions you are willing to take to achieve your goals. They are the foundation for objective decision making, and they help determine strategies, activities, and resources for continuous improvement. When collective commitments are used to drive decision making, budgetary decisions are made more objectively. They allow schools to prioritize needs and move away from doing things simply because "that's the way they have always been done." In addition, collective commitments can act as a filtering tool for human resources and should be shared with all potential candidates to ensure understanding and alignment.

Here are our school's collective commitments:

- We believe in the power of positive relationships. We commit to creating a caring and safe environment and allowing a fresh start every day.
- We believe in providing the highest-quality learning experiences for our students. We commit to maintaining high expectations, using data to drive our decision making, and implementing systems that help make every child successful.
- We believe that effective school improvement is a collaborative culture focused on student learning. We commit to collaborating effectively, putting the team before individuals, encouraging and supporting one another, and holding one another accountable.
- We believe in embracing change. We commit to accepting challenges with a growth mindset.

After this process, we had new banners made for our lobby, cafeteria, and library, and we made posters for each classroom. (See Figure 1.2.) Our shared mission, vision, and collective commitments were now an integral part of the fiber of our school; therefore, we made sure to make them visible to anyone entering our building. Placing these statements in each classroom also increased student awareness.

Having the Courage to Say *No* So Your Teachers Will Say *Yes*

As leaders, we make hundreds of decisions each day, including dozens of must-dos and may-dos. Without a clear understanding of where they are going and what they are willing to do to get there, leaders sometimes get lost in the weeds of decision making and end up saying *yes* to things that may seem like a good opportunity in the moment—but are not actually in alignment with the school's mission and vision.

When you are crystal clear about who you are, where you are going, and how you will get there, you are in a good position not only to say *yes* to the things that are best for your school but also to say *no* to the things that could potentially cloud the vision and derail your goals. You're also armed with a solid rationale and defense for why you chose to say *no* in the face of a strong push from your district to adopt "the next best thing."

FIGURE: 1.2
Example Vision Statement, Mission Statement, and Collective Commitments

---

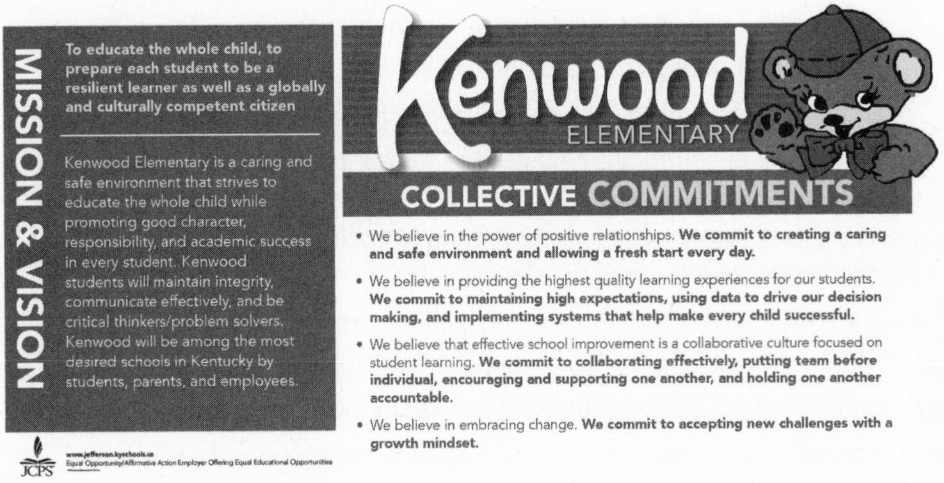

Having a leader who understood the need to gain staff voice and feedback to establish a shared vision would have helped support decision making around the adoption of a new curriculum in the elementary school at the beginning of this chapter. Leaders who push forward with initiatives despite a lack of staff voice and readiness risk inhibiting coherence, increasing staff frustration, and stifling change.

Think about the last time your school engaged in a new initiative. Was that initiative filtered through the lens of an alignment with your mission, vision, and collective commitments, or was it pushed through in a way that left staff feeling overwhelmed and undervalued?

A shared mission and vision allow your school to be crystal clear about who you are, what you believe, and where you are going—and collective commitments provide a map for getting there. Your core values define your school's moral compass, and identifying your *why* provides inspiration to live up to those values. When leaders collaborate with their staff, they create synergy around a common goal and objectively drive decision making in a way that helps teachers stay focused and inspired.

If your staff were asked the following questions, would they all answer in a similar way?

- Why do you (as a school) exist?
- What drives your decision making?
- What is your North Star?

If the answer is *yes*, all teachers are currently on the same page, then you are already ahead of many organizations. What evidence of your *why* can be seen and heard at your school? When your *why* drives your actions, it can be seen, heard, and felt by anyone who enters your building. When people feel supported and protected in an organization, they develop trust and loyalty and are more likely to put in the extra effort that benefits the entire organization. Sinek (2009) reminds us, "When people come to work with a higher sense of purpose, they find it easier to weather hard times or even find opportunity in those hard times" (p. 101). In the end, your *why* will keep staff united and inspired, and the *what* and *how* provide clarity and reduce frustration. To combat teacher burnout, you need all three.

Think-Abouts

1. What is your *why*, and when was the last time you reflected on it?
2. How have you engaged your staff in reflecting on their *why*?
3. In what ways have you engaged in a process to identify your core values?
4. How does your school's mission statement reflect your school's values and beliefs about why you exist?

5. Does your school's vision statement establish where you want to be? What steps have you taken to ensure it is realistic and achievable?

6. How did you ensure your mission and vision statements were developed collaboratively with all stakeholders?

7. How did you involve all stakeholders to ensure your collective commitments include actionable steps that target your goals?

2

The Gift of Time

"The truth is that teamwork is at the heart of great achievement."

—John C. Maxwell

> **🔋 Burnout Challenge**
>
> To meet the diverse needs of all students, teachers are being asked to add more and more elements (e.g., differentiation, cultural relevance, student choice) to their unit and lesson plans, but they don't have adequate planning and preparation time.

It was after midnight when Mr. Hayes finally closed his laptop. He had been providing individual feedback to each of his students on their most recent social studies project for the last three hours and had hit a wall. As he lay in bed trying to sleep, he kept thinking about everything he still needed to do. Although his lesson plans for the rest of this week were complete, his team had not had time to meet to look at their next unit (which would begin the following week). In addition, he still needed to complete a counseling referral for two of his students, prepare for an upcoming IEP meeting for another student, and finish the family newsletter that was to go home the following day. When Mr. Hayes woke up the next morning, he felt tired, anxious, and overwhelmed. It should come as no surprise that he is not alone. In fact, a heavier workload and poor work-life balance are primary factors leading to higher stress and burnout (Darbishire et al., 2020).

Collaboration Is Key

Teaching is hard work. Trying to do everything alone will quickly lead to burnout. In addition to all the roles teachers juggle on a daily basis to meet the complex needs of their students, compassion fatigue intensifies when teachers remain isolated in silos. The truth is that to meet the diverse needs of all students, teachers are required to add more and more elements (e.g., differentiation, cultural relevance, student choice) to their unit and lesson plans, but they don't have adequate planning and preparation time. With all the responsibilities teachers have on their plates right now, if we as leaders expect to see the impact of collective efficacy, then we must work to create the conditions that provide collaborative time. Sometimes the opportunities are embedded (such as common planning), but other times you have to be more creative. In addition to providing time for teachers, we must also understand the conditions necessary for effective collaboration and ensure we are creating those conditions in our schools.

Some of the basal elements of effective collaboration are trust and mutual respect. When was the last time you were completely vulnerable and open with a group just because you work with them? Most likely your answer is never. However, teachers are often expected to mesh immediately with their teammates and produce great things, even though trust is developed over time and through deliberate relationship building. Relational trust is formed through personal interactions and involves the display of core values such as "respect, competence, personal regard for others, and integrity" (Bryck & Schneider, 2002, p. 23). Therefore, if we expect our teachers to build trusting relationships with one another, then we must also be intentional about creating the conditions that make those relationships possible.

To ensure this, make sure you dedicate intentional time for team building (more about this in Chapter 8) and build in time throughout the year for teams to have deliberate time together to strengthen their bond. Teams must be intentional about establishing norms and goals for themselves, and leaders must be intentional about making sure they recognize and celebrate teams when they reach those goals. What opportunities are you providing for staff to develop these dispositions with one another?

Remember that time is one of the most valuable resources you can provide your teachers. Collaboration sets the stage for co-planning and co-teaching, which leads to significant educational impact with calibrated teacher expectations, teacher clarity, and strong classroom cohesion—providing more equitable access and opportunity for the students in your school (Hattie, 2019). Keep in mind, however, that even though collaboration is an essential element of school improvement and effective practices, collaboration without an intentional focus on the right work will not have the intended impact. If teachers feel as though they are meeting to check a compliance expectation for their administrators, they will probably feel like more has been added to their plate—instead of having something taken off it. This chapter includes some of the ways we provide intentional collaborative time for our staff to ensure they feel supported and develop collective efficacy, which garners the largest effect size (1.57) on student achievement (Hattie, 2019).

Master Schedule

As a visionary leader, you must keep an eye on the big picture and create systems and structures that work interdependently of one another. To that end, the master schedule is *everything*. One of its greatest advantages is the collaborative opportunities it provides. For example, the master schedule allows us to add an additional layer of support for all students and teachers in the form of additional staff who can help implement small-group instruction. This includes the intentional use of English language development (ELD) teachers, special education (SE) teachers, and instructional assistants. Struggle with content is one of the biggest causes of adverse student behaviors (Mitchell et al., 2018), so adding this layer of academic support is one of the most effective proactive supports we have implemented to decrease disruptive behaviors. Although that was not the initial intent of the master schedule, the impact it has had on decreasing disruptive behaviors in our building is undeniable.

If you are not currently in charge of your school's master schedule, then there may be some initial resistance because, truthfully, a master schedule that truly honors collaboration and support for an entire building cannot honor the individualized needs of each teacher. Therefore, it is critical that you create and cultivate a culture that honors collaboration and teamwork. When I (Jill) first began to create my school's master schedule, I asked staff to list the top three priorities they had in a schedule. Some of the priorities that emerged were extra support during math workshop, continuation of the reading lab, and dedicated WIN (what I need) time. Next, I asked each grade level to provide me with a copy of what they considered their ideal schedule. With those two pieces of information, I set out to create a master schedule that included the top three identified priorities and honored at least one component of everyone's ideal schedule. Although creating a master schedule is often like navigating a giant game of Tetris, it will be worth every hour you spend on it.

When the master schedule is created with such intentionality, it sets the tone for the other schedules in the building. Special education services, English as a second language (ESL) programming, and other intervention schedules can be designed with individual students' needs in mind to ensure that multiple data points and areas of focus are tightly aligned and to confirm students receive the support that maximizes their learning opportunities. Co-teaching is possible when co-planning exists. In addition to creating schedules that integrate collaborative opportunities for teachers and students, it is also important to ensure general education teachers share common planning times with ELD and SE teachers with whom they share students. It is during these times that ELD and SE teachers make recommendations and intentionally embed scaffolds and supports for lessons. During common planning time, collaborative partners should also discuss student progress data and determine instructional next steps for acceleration, intervention, and enrichment. Figure 2.1 shows a sample master schedule, and Figure 2.2 shows a sample schedule for an ELD teacher.

Common Planning

One of the must-haves in our master schedule is common planning time for teams of teachers. Effective collaboration is hard to achieve when teachers don't have time in the workday to meet with one another. Although common planning is essential, leaders must also create a culture that values collaboration. When teachers experience the unlimited benefits of a professional learning community (PLC), they will never know how they functioned before that. PLCs, as defined by Hord (1997), are groups where teachers can investigate how to improve their practice together and take collective responsibility for implementing what they discover. This idea was transformed into a specific approach to collective team meetings in which teams establish clear goals, promote team building, gather data, undertake problem solving, and design interventions (DuFour et al., 2010). To clarify exactly what students are expected to learn and to monitor each student's learning progress, PLCs should focus on the following four questions:

- What do we want all students to know and be able to do?
- How will we know if they learn it?
- How will we respond when some students do not learn?
- How will we extend the learning for students who are already proficient?

The tenets of these four questions seem simple enough, but there is a greater level of sophistication required to develop a highly functioning PLC. Our school was fortunate enough to be selected as a pilot school to

FIGURE 2.1
Example of a K–3 Master Schedule

Kindergarten	1st	2nd	3rd
MM 9:00–9:30 K Teacher - ELD Teacher K Teacher - ELD Teacher K Teacher - ELD Teacher K Teacher - ELD Teacher	MM 9:00–9:30	MM 9:00–9:20	MM 9:00–9:30
			9:30–9:50 Mini Lesson (ELD teacher possible newcomer group)
			9:50–10:50 Special Area
9:30–11:00 Reading K Teacher - Instructional Assistant + Special Education Teacher 9:45–10:45 K Teacher - Instructional Assistant K Teacher - Instructional Assistant K Teacher - Instructional Assistant + Special Education Teacher 9:30–10:30	9:30–11:00 Math 1st Grade Teacher - ELD Teacher 1st Grade Teacher - Bilingual Associate Instructor 1st Grade Teacher - Instructional Assistant 1st Grade Teacher - Bilingual Associate Instructor	9:20–10:50 Reading/Math Reading 2nd Grade Teacher - ELD Teacher 2nd Grade Teacher - Instructional Assistant Math 2nd Grade Teacher - Bilingual Associate Instructor 2nd Grade Teacher - Bilingual Associate Instructor	10:50–11:50 Reading/Math 3rd Grade Classrooms A & B Reading 3rd Grade Teacher - ELD Teacher 3rd Grade Teacher - Instructional Assistant Math 3rd Grade Teacher - N/A 3rd Grade Teacher - Bilingual Associate Instructor
11:00–12:00 Lunch/Writing/Phonics	11:00–11:20 Phonics 11:20–12:00 Lunch/Writing 1st Grade Teacher - ELD Teacher	10:55–11:55 Special Area	

Kindergarten	1st	2nd	3rd
12:00–1:25 Math	12:00–1:00 Special Area	11:55–1:10 Writing & Lunch	11:50–1:05 Lunch/Writing
K assistants until 1:20		2nd Grade Teacher - ELD Teacher	3rd Grade Teacher - ELD Teacher
K Teacher - Bilingual Associate Instructor	1:00–3:00 Reading		
K Teacher - Bilingual Associate Instructor	Shared Reading & 4 Groups	1:10–2:40 Reading/Math	1:05–2:30 Reading
K Teacher - Special Education Teacher Bilingual Associate Instructor	1st Grade Teacher - Instructional Assistant	Reading	Reading
K Teacher - Bilingual Associate Instructor	1st Grade Teacher - Instructional Assistant	2nd Grade Teacher - ELD Teacher	3rd Grade Teacher - ELD Teacher
12:20–1:20	1st Grade Teacher - Instructional Assistant	2nd Grade Teacher - Instructional Assistant	3rd Grade Teacher - Instructional Assistant
	1st Grade Teacher - Instructional Assistant Special Education Teacher	Math	Math
1:25–2:25 Special Area		2nd Grade Teacher - Bilingual Associate Instructor	3rd Grade Teacher - Bilingual Associate Instructor
	1:20–2:25	2nd Grade Teacher - Bilingual Associate Instructor	3rd Grade Teacher - Bilingual Associate Instructor
2:25–3:00 Writing/Phonics	ELD Teacher - pull language groups	2:40–3:10 Wellness	2:30–3:00 Wellness
3:00–3:30 Wellness	3:00–3:30 Wellness	3:10–3:30 Phonics	3:00–3:30 WN 3rd Grade Teacher - ELD Teacher
3:30–3:45 RA	3:30–3:45 RA	3:30–3:45 RA	3:30–3:45 RA

Note: "ELD Teacher" stands for English language development teachers providing ESL services.

FIGURE 2.2
Example of ELD Teacher Schedule

Time/Location	Grade	Program Model	Content Focus	Homeroom Teacher	Monday	Tuesday	Wednesday	Thursday	Friday
8:30–9:00	N/A				Morning Duty-Gym				
9:00–9:25	2	Pull-out	Language (based on MAP needs)	Teacher 1	Flex, makeup, assessment	Wonderful Student (2.9)		Superstar Student (3.2)	
						Amazing Student (2.0)		Amazing Student (3.7)	
						Strong Student (3.0)		Outstanding Student (2.6)	
9:25–9:50	2	Pull-out (Push-in on Monday)	Language (based on MAP needs)	Teacher 1, Teacher 2, Teacher 3, Teacher 4	Student 1 (3.3)	Student 6 (2.5)		Student 10 (2.0)	
					Student 2 (3.2)	Student 7 (3.7)		Student 11 (1.7)	
					Student 3 (3.3)	Student 8 (3.1)		Student 12 (2.8)	
9:50–10:50	1	Push-in	Reading Lab	Teacher 5, Teacher 6, Teacher 7, Teacher 8	Student Names & ACCESS Scores				
10:50–11:20	1	Pull-out	Language (based on MAP needs)	Teacher 5, Teacher 6, Teacher 7, Teacher 8	Rotate groups/ Flex Day	Student Names & ACCESS Scores			

Time/Location	Grade	Program Model	Content Focus	Homeroom Teacher	Monday	Tuesday	Wednesday	Thursday	Friday
11:20–11:50	5	Pull-out	Intermediate Newcomer Support	Teacher 9, Teacher 10	Student Names & ACCESS Scores				
11:50–12:10					Lunch				
12:10–1:10					Planning				
1:10–1:35	2	Pull-out	Literacy Lessons	Teacher 2	Superstar Reader (2.5)				
1:35–2:00	2	Pull-out	Primary Newcomer Support	Teacher 3, Teacher 7	Student Names & ACCESS Scores				
2:00–3:00	2	Push-in	Reading Lab	Teacher 1, Teacher 2, Teacher 3, Teacher 4	Student Names & ACCESS Scores				
3:00–3:30 (M–Th)	3	Push-in		Teacher 12	Student Names & ACCESS Scores				Clubs (2:30–3:30)

train in this process. The training lasted for three years, and even though it was incredibly rigorous, it changed the way we approached teaching and learning—and in just three years, our students' math proficiency tripled. In addition to increasing student achievement, this professional learning also reduced feelings of isolation and enhanced the collective efficacy of our staff. Teachers began to value the power of collaboration and had higher motivation and satisfaction for the job.

When schools put in the work, both students and staff win. We have experienced great success as a result of our PLC work; however, we must caution you about some of the pitfalls you need to avoid:

- PLCs should be administratively supported rather than administratively driven. You want teachers to own the data and make data-driven instructional shifts that support attainment of mastery for all students. If you are dictating agenda items and controlling the conversation, the ownership stays with you. To demonstrate the value you ascribe to PLCs, we suggest administrative attendance at all collaborative team meetings. When engaging in conversations with teachers, do so to clarify, consult, or celebrate. Try to develop a culture in which team leaders are responsible for creating the agendas and ensuring necessary data are available for each meeting. Instructional coaches should be available to support if needed, but it is essential to empower your teachers.
- Do not criticize in meetings. Highly functioning teams are those with members who have developed trust and can be vulnerable with one another. Criticism and control from administrators can shut this down and minimize the potential impact of the team.
- A PLC is who you are—not what you do. It is critical to help staff understand this.

When teachers see PLCs as part of the ingrained culture and not just a collection of compliance meetings, there is a shift from thinking about *my* students to *our* students. They understand the value of a team and the impact of collective efficacy. Shared responsibility increases the team's productivity and decreases the siloed workload of individual teachers. In essence, it provides more time for teachers because they are not doing everything by themselves.

In addition to grade or subject groups meeting together, this structure provides support staff, such as ELD and SE teachers, with time and opportunity to meet and provide scaffolds for instruction, analyze disaggregated data, and provide embedded professional development.

Unit Planning Days

Although daily common planning time provides designated opportunities for student work and data analysis that can ultimately lead to instructional decision making about interventions, enrichment, and acceleration, deep dives into standards and thorough unit plan development require longer spans of uninterrupted time. Every year, one of our budgetary priorities is providing dedicated unit planning days to teams. When teachers have uninterrupted time to collaborate with one another, they can intentionally create units through a backward design model—which provides insight into students' progression toward mastery, helps teachers measure the impact of instruction, and guides instructional decision making.

What does this look like in practice? Teams begin with the end in mind and create

- Pre-assessments to review prior skills and consider possible misconceptions.
- Common standards-based assessments.
- Daily formative assessments.
- Performance assessment opportunities.
- Assessment rubrics so students have clear expectations.

They then create daily lessons that include

- Lesson frames to use when tracking mastery of daily goals (e.g., *I can...*).
- Opportunities to activate background knowledge and provide experience to help students anchor new learning.
- A plan to address misconceptions.
- Minilessons with clear checkpoints.

Finally, teams ensure that each unit includes multiple opportunities to

- Include diverse cultural perspectives.
- Consider the progression of standards to track student success and mastery.
- Engage in higher-level cognitive tasks.
- Demonstrate learning.
- Apply 21st century skills.
- Engage an authentic audience and make real-world connections.
- Extend the lesson for more proficient students.

Unfortunately, because of teacher shortages in our district (which is, admittedly, a universal phenomenon), providing substitutes to secure these unit planning days was prohibited in the wake of the COVID-19 pandemic (even though we had budgeted for it). Knowing the value this time had for our teachers, not having unit planning days was simply not an option for us. Therefore, we had to be creative with our plans and utilize staff in a way that still made this valuable opportunity possible.

We brought the assistant principal, mental health practitioner, counselor, and compassion teacher on board and had them rotate among the classes and each provide an hour of instruction that focused on social-emotional and social justice needs. This coverage, combined with the teachers' own planning time, came to five hours of uninterrupted unit planning time. Even though it didn't completely mirror the full-day unit planning we had in the past, it still provided valuable extended planning time, engaged students in SEL support, and didn't cost the school any unbudgeted funding.

When conducting a needs assessment with our teachers, unit planning days rated high on their list of needs. Therefore, we knew that we must overcome any obstacle that stood in the way and had the potential to derail our plans. What items are at the top of your needs assessment? How are you making sure those needs don't get derailed?

Special-Area Schedule

We make sure our master schedule includes blocks for special-area classes (to guarantee teams have common planning time). Therefore, we suggest that you analyze your current special-area schedule to ensure you are also making the most of any open blocks your teachers may have. When determining how best to utilize this time, it's a good idea to revisit your school's mission, vision, and needs assessment. Over the years, we have utilized special-area blocks for a variety of purposes, including extra planning for individual teachers and push-in interventions for reading and math. As our needs changed over time, we found that utilizing the blocks to support student enrichment—while also supporting teacher growth and development—has given us the biggest bang for the buck. This is a structure we call Individualized Professional Development, or IPD Days.

In Chapter 5, we discuss our structure for supporting teachers through coaching, counseling, peer observations, and individualized professional development. Although we have instituted the individual components of this system over the years, creating a master schedule that allows for it all to take place during the same day has been a game changer. Giving teachers the gift of time—namely, almost an entire day every six weeks to focus on themselves—has been invaluable. At first, teachers were concerned about missing time with their students, but after their first IPD day, the feedback we received about how refreshed and renewed they felt was overwhelming. The plan stuck.

Collaborative Conversations

Creating a master schedule to provide common planning for teams of teachers is possible, but there may still be a gap in communication and collaboration between teachers and support staff and interventionists. In many schools, support staff and interventionists work with students across multiple grade levels, making it impossible for them to attend common planning time for all the grades they serve. Because collaborative time with homeroom teachers, when they can discuss student progress, is so valuable, we specifically developed opportunities for these conversations to take place. After teams administer a common assessment, they sign up for a collaborative conversation time slot on our school's living calendar. These are 30-minute blocks of time for teachers to meet with their interventionists to analyze data and determine instructional next steps.

Integrated Systems

Let's face it, time is in limited supply and is not something we can ever increase. We must therefore create conditions that optimize the time we have. Unless we are intentional about establishing integrated systems, teachers will see everything they are required to do—no matter how important—as "one more thing" on their plate. As leaders, we are required to see everything we do through a systems lens. How do all the tasks we require of teachers overlap, and how can we streamline the approach? Every school has its own set of nuances, but the overarching categories shown in Figure 2.3 are ones that most schools share.

Part of our administrative retreat each year focuses on conducting a systems analysis to determine what we need to keep doing and what we need to revise to better support our goals and vision. To analyze the impact and effectiveness of each system, we look at each category, rank ourselves 1 (novice) through 4 (distinguished), and determine who will oversee that system. When assigning leadership oversight, we try to align responsibilities with each team member's role and strengths. Because stakeholder

FIGURE 2.3

Categories for Integrated Systems

Operations	Curriculum & Instruction	Family & Community Engagement	Climate & Culture	Coaching & Development	Human Resources
Finance & Budget	PLC Process	MTSS for Families	School Environment	Professional Development	Staffing
Safety & Emergency Procedures	Data Collection & Analysis	PTO/PTA	PBIS	Coaching	Evaluations
Building & Grounds	Academic MTSS	Community Events	MTSS for Behavior	Feedback Loop Visits	Intensive Support
Food Services	Curricular Resources	Conference Day	Schoolwide Expectations	Individualized Professional Development (IPD)	Attraction & Retention
Graduation	Common Assessments	Community Partnerships	Mental Health Supports	Co-planning and Modeling Lessons	Equity
Transportation	Deconstruction of Standards	Home Visits	Equity	Equity	
Building Assessment Coordinator (ACT, SAT, district and state assessments)	Instructional Leadership Team	Volunteers			
Equity	Equity	Equity			

input helps drive our decision making, we also provide opportunities for systems feedback with the rest of our staff—and family and community partners. As you reflect on these categories, consider how effective your systems are for each, and think about what measures you have put in place to ensure they are interconnected.

Recall Mr. Hayes's feelings of exhaustion from the beginning of this chapter. By being intentional with your school's schedules, collaborative opportunities, and resources, you can create conditions that decrease the likelihood of your teachers having a similar response to "not having enough time." To provide opportunities like the ones mentioned in this chapter and your teachers the gift of time, you must be strategic with your budget and resources and think outside the box.

Think-Abouts

1. On a scale from 1 to 10, how would you rate the culture of collaboration in your school?
2. How are you creating opportunities for teams to develop trust and mutual respect for one another?
3. As a leader, what is your role in creating the master schedule?
4. How has your master schedule been aligned to ensure teams of teachers have common planning time?
5. How are you being creative with your resources to provide time for unit planning?
6. How are you providing intentional time for interventionist and support staff to meet with homeroom and content teachers to ensure co-planning opportunities exist?
7. When was the last time you conducted an analysis of your current systems?

3

Effective Communication

"Effective communication requires more than an exchange of information.
When done right, communication fosters understanding, strengthens
relationships, improves teamwork, and builds trust."

—Liz Papadopoulos

> **[□□ ▷ Burnout Challenge**
>
> Unclear expectations, ineffective and inconsistent communication, and lack of information leads to teachers feeling frustrated because they spend unnecessary time searching for emails, planning documents, events, and more instead of focusing on their students.

Ms. Johnson, a 7th grade science teacher at Pleasantville Middle School, found herself frustrated by the lack of effective communication between teachers and administrators at her school. Some teachers seemed to know everything about what was going on, yet others felt totally out of the loop. Ideas and concerns seemed to get lost in a sea of bureaucracy, which hindered collaboration, prevented progress, and stifled innovation. In addition, there was no structure for teachers to have their voices heard, which led to a small minority of staff speaking for everyone. Communication between administrators and teachers was sporadic and inconsistent, resulting in a lack of transparency that inhibited clarity and a common understanding of the goals and activities needed to move toward a shared vision.

Other teachers on the science team complained to Ms. Johnson—the school's union representative—about the time they had to spend looking for communication, forms, and planning documents because of the ineffective systems for communication that existed at their school. Ms. Johnson was desperate to enact change that would lead to clear and consistent communication practices, and she and her colleagues are certainly not alone in their frustration and desperation.

Ineffective communication—which ultimately creates dissonance, confusion, and a lack of transparency—is another top reason teachers leave the profession (Luhombo et al., 2023). When leaders fail to communicate effectively, it leaves employees confused and can create an atmosphere of anxiety and distrust. Having a breakdown in, or total absence of, communication between leaders and their staff can also result in hindered teamwork and a lack of collegiality (Marzano et al., 2005; Newton, 2015).

By contrast, effective communication promotes motivation and builds staff culture (Tyler, 2016). Martinez and Hurtado (2018) posit that effective internal communication is vital to clearly articulate an organization's values, goals, and objectives and to inspire positive outcomes with staff. When leaders communicate effectively with their staff, it can lead to increased job satisfaction and reduced teacher turnover (Ali et al., 2021). In short, it is critical to ensure that everyone stays focused and on the same page regarding the continuing work of the school. When a leader communicates effectively, it removes the frustration that emerges when teachers have to "waste time looking for information," freeing up more time to focus on the work that has the most impact on students.

Effective communication is clear, consistent, concise, and contains the elements of trust, transparency, and active listening (Salamondra, 2021). We contend that effective communication also includes an element of compassion. When determining the purpose and audience of your communication, it is important to keep all these considerations in mind. Brené Brown (2018) reminds us that *clear is kind and unclear is unkind* when referencing the way in which we lead and communicate with others. She also stresses the need to ensure our communication clearly articulates exactly what we want it to say while "fostering curiosity, learning, collaboration, reality checking, and ultimately success" (p. 102).

The goal of communication should be to provide a clear understanding of the goals and expectations of your organization so everyone is on the same page. According to Garcia and Weiss (2019), the main reasons teachers are leaving the profession can be organized into four categories: barriers to teaching, stress and physical safety, lack of support by administration, and low satisfaction, motivation, and expectations.

With that in mind, this chapter focuses on how leaders can combat low satisfaction, motivation, and expectations. We understand that when a school year gets off to a tumultuous start, there may be a need to address immediate concerns—to stop the bleeding, as it were. However, it is also important to stay focused on the big picture and keep building a long-term plan for success. This chapter includes ways not only to triage with immediate action but also to develop systems and structures that sustain the work over the long term.

Living Calendar

When I (Jill) first became a teacher, my principal reviewed expectations about "how to sign up" for spaces and places. If, for example, I wanted to use the auditorium or plan a field trip, I would need to consult the full wall-size calendar in the front office and claim the space and place by writing my intentions (e.g., 5th grade field trip to the zoo). Interestingly enough, when I became a principal years later at a different school, the same protocols and procedures existed there.

My guess is this sounds very familiar to you since I am pretty sure a giant wall calendar used to come with the keys to the school building. Don't get me wrong—as a systems thinker, I appreciate having a protocol for things. The problem with this protocol, however, is that the minute I walked away, the calendar became outdated—not to mention how inconvenient it was to have all schoolwide events tracked in a location with limited access.

To combat this issue, we transitioned to a living calendar. A living calendar can, as the name implies, be updated in real time and is available to everyone. We create our calendar as a simple table in Google Docs. (Our academic coach changes the background and adds graphics to make it more aesthetically appealing.) All staff members are granted editing access, and one of their check-out procedures before the end of the school year is to add their birthday to the calendar. This ensures they know how to find, bookmark, and add to the calendar.

To make sure our systems work with one another, we proactively schedule all our faculty meetings, emergency drills, professional development days, family engagement events, and anything else that affects the entire school prior to the start of the school year. As the year progresses, this tool becomes a major means of schoolwide communication and includes links to things such as PLC agendas and weekly newsletters from coaches and administrators. Our goal with the living calendar is to create a one-stop shop that communicates all the internal happenings at our school.

"Whom to Go to for What"

We believe in empowering others through distributive leadership that builds on the strengths of the staff. To that end, a roles and responsibilities list for each member of the administrative team helps ensure clarity of expectations. However, it could also become overwhelming for staff if there's an expectation that they need to remember what everyone is responsible for. Therefore, we created a "Whom to Go to for What" document that includes a photo of each staff member along with a list of primary roles and responsibilities and pertinent links. This document, along with several others, is linked at the bottom of our living calendar. Figure 3.1 shows a sample of the principal's section.

FIGURE 3.1 **Whom to Go to for What**		
Contact	**Support/Forms/Resources**	
Principal	• Student Shout Out Form • Kenwood 2.0 • PGP Form • Master Schedule • Lunch Schedule • Support Staff Schedule • Pledge • Wellness • Special Area • Beginning of the Year Forms • ESL Schedule • Scheduling Questions • ILT • SBDM • Kentucky Code of Ethics	• Job Descriptions • Coaching • Classified/Certified Evaluations • Certified Evaluation Plan • Certified Evaluation Forms • Certified Evaluation Process • Certified Summative Evaluation Schedule • Certified Evaluation Forms • Evaluation Overview • End of the Year Checkout Lists • IPD • IFS of a Great Lesson • Peer Observations • Guess Who Form • Collaboration Check List

Weekly Communication

Another thing we have learned is that you can never overcommunicate. As the building leader, you most likely send out some form of weekly communication. Here are some tips we've found useful when crafting these weekly messages:

- **Consistency:** If possible, try to send your communication on the same day and at the same time each week. Maybe you send a newsletter on Friday evenings so staff will have it for the following week. The rationale here is sound, but after discussions with many principals, general consensus is that most staff members just want to relax on the weekend—and the newsletter is an unnecessary stressor. Therefore, you may want to consider linking your newsletter (or other form of communication) to a living calendar on Sunday afternoon and then sending the update email to staff on Monday morning. Doing this allows anyone who wants to access it on Sunday the opportunity to do so, but it won't deliver directly to anyone until Monday morning.

- **Less Is More:** If there are multiple newsletters sent out per week, consider if they're all absolutely necessary. Sending more than two or three newsletters to staff (e.g., one from the principal and one from the assistant principal) can be overwhelming. Think of ways to combine your newsletters to amplify their impact and to make the message more meaningful and less overwhelming to read.

- **Celebrations and Recognitions:** Public celebrations are a great way to recognize individuals and teams for their accomplishments, extra service, or risk taking. In Chapter 7, we discuss additional ways to demonstrate appreciation of and with your staff.

- **Weekly Calendar:** Updates taken from the living calendar can provide staff with a weekly at-a-glance view of the events that will impact them or the entire school community.

- **Updates:** Updates that come from the district office ensure staff members are staying abreast of what is happening not only at their school but also at the district level.

- **Article of the Week:** If providing ongoing professional development for your staff is a priority, then link a professional "article of the week" to your weekly communication. Try to identify articles on topics that relate to issues and challenges that were uncovered through PLC and coaching conversations.

- **Think-Abouts:** Do you want your teachers to be reflective practitioners? If so, then you should include questions in your weekly newsletter for them to reflect upon. Often, these questions relate to the article of the week, but they can also focus on instructional practices or trends you have observed in classrooms or collaborative team meetings.

- **Quotes:** Who doesn't love a good quote to get them through the week? Consider including relevant and inspirational quotes in your weekly communication and living calendar.

Other considerations to keep in mind include the format and medium you want to use to communicate. People communicate differently, so you might want to try releasing your weekly message in multiple formats (e.g., written, video, screencast with slide deck to highlight main points). One of my colleagues, Courtney Grace, utilizes Google Sites (a structured web page creation tool within the Google suite) for her weekly message and embeds the following components within her weekly communication: master calendar, staff spotlight, principal's message, educational articles or videos, school attendance percentages, school quick links, and district updates. Courtney does a really great job threading the school's core values throughout all components of her weekly message.

Weekly communication should be both informative and encouraging—not overwhelming—so if you send multiple messages (perhaps along with other leaders), come up with a schedule to stagger your messages. Maybe one person sends out a weekly newsletter (Mindset Monday) on Monday morning, another sends out a message (Wellness Wednesday) midweek on Wednesday, and a third sends out a final message (Fab Friday) on Friday morning. Important notifications should be repeated in all three newsletters to ensure consistency, but each message should have a different primary purpose and use a different medium. For example, Mindset Monday has a strong instructional focus and utilizes Google Docs, Wellness Wednesday focuses on daily sustainability and staff well-being and incorporates a lot of videos, and Fab Friday covers operational needs and upcoming events using Google Slides.

Emails

Email is one of the greatest forms of communication because it is so efficient. That being said, it is really important to construct your emails so people will not open them and immediately back out—or automatically delete them. Here are some recommendations for effective and thoughtful use of email communication:

- Be clear and concise as much as possible.
- Send emails during work hours or schedule them so they are delivered during work hours.
- Respond to all emails within 24 hours, even if it is just a quick note to let the sender know you have received and are working on their request.
- If you must send an email outside work hours—because of extenuating circumstances such as an emergency or safety concerns—text team leaders letting them know the email has been sent and needs to be attended to immediately so they can relay pertinent information to the rest of their team.
- Think before you reply. It is difficult to accurately detect tone via written text, and you want to minimize misunderstanding or miscommunication.
- If the content of your email is confidential or of a sensitive nature, make a phone call instead.
- Reply All should be used *very* rarely—and only when absolutely necessary.

Google Workspace

You may already know everything there is to know about Google Workspace. For everyone else, say hello to one of the most beneficial tools for organizing all the documents you use throughout the school year. Our school heavily relies on the use of Google apps to communicate with staff. Google Workspace, however, is so much more than a simple vehicle for weekly communication. In Chapter 2, we talked about the importance of collaboration and the impact it can have on collective teacher efficacy. If teachers are going to collaborate with one another, they must have access to the same resources and planning documents. Having each team create a shared folder accessible by the entire staff increases opportunities for co-planning and co-teaching since multiple people can access and edit the same document without disrupting the flow of the task they are working on. Using a common shared set of tools also enhances communication because of your ability to store, organize, and locate necessary documents relevant to meeting minutes, agendas, and so much more.

Meeting Structures

Newsletters and emails are an effective way to deliver information to your staff, but they don't invite communication and collaboration in a way that face-to-face meetings (both in-person and virtual) can. That said, valuing your staff's time is paramount. Therefore, meetings that could have been an email or memo should be avoided at all costs. Meetings should be used to develop your staff professionally or create a forum in which you gain insight and invite teachers to collaborate. When scheduling meetings, it is important you are intentional about the ways in which you organize and structure them. In addition to distributive leadership, our school, for example, also follows a collaborative leadership model. Figure 3.2 provides a visual of how we structure our meetings to ensure stakeholder feedback and consistency in messaging.

Agendas

An effective meeting structure can help ensure consistency of messaging to all stakeholders, but having a well-thought-out agenda promotes intentionality of content and provides clarity to ensure the meeting adheres to the given timeframe and topic. We suggest that you send agendas to all participants at least 48 hours ahead of time to allow everyone an opportunity to mentally prepare for the topic and gather any necessary resources. Additional time also allows other stakeholders the opportunity to contribute important items relevant to their role.

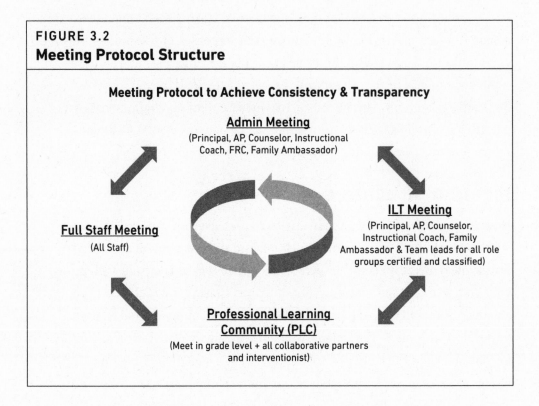

FIGURE 3.2
Meeting Protocol Structure

Meeting Protocol to Achieve Consistency & Transparency

Admin Meeting
(Principal, AP, Counselor, Instructional Coach, FRC, Family Ambassador)

ILT Meeting
(Principal, AP, Counselor, Instructional Coach, Family Ambassador & Team leads for all role groups certified and classified)

Full Staff Meeting
(All Staff)

Professional Learning Community (PLC)
(Meet in grade level + all collaborative partners and interventionist)

Agendas should never be created on the spot or during the meeting. Doing this demonstrates a lack of respect for the participants and hints at your lack of preparedness. Figure 3.3 is a sample outline of the way we structure our agendas. We have found that, in addition to collectively established group norms, highlighting goals for every meeting allows participants to clearly see how the content of the meeting aligns with team and school goals. We always start team meetings with a quick review of the calendar to ensure everyone is on the same page with respect to expectations around upcoming events. Including who is responsible for various agenda items provides an opportunity for stakeholder engagement beyond the moderator/leader, and the estimated time ensures we stay on track and that no one agenda item consumes the entire meeting. This agenda template also assists with follow-up, accountability, and planning for future meetings.

FIGURE 3.3
Agenda Template

Agenda				
Department/Team Goals:				
Group Norms:				
Living Calendar				
Responsible Party & Time Allotment	**Agenda Item**	**Goal(s) Addressed**	**Notes**	**Follow-Up Needed**

Maintaining digital agendas has not only helped us become more ecologically responsible but also allowed us to maintain live minutes from each meeting for everyone to access. To further streamline meeting communication, we link our meeting agendas/minutes to the living calendar. This provides a one-stop shop for the entire staff, and it also acts as a resource hub that tells the story of your school's work.

Onboarding New Staff

In addition to ensuring clear and consistent communication with your staff, it is also important to think about ways in which you will onboard new staff. Do you have a protocol in place to welcome new staff members and help them get acclimated to your school's culture? At our school, new staff members are welcomed with an informative email along with a "welcome to our school" goody bag. They also participate in a scavenger hunt (created by our academic instructional coach, Brandee Kaelin) that introduces them to different staff members with whom they will be communicating and helps them acclimate to the different systems and structures we have. Providing this before they begin—or before school starts—helps reduce anxiety for new teachers by establishing a clearly defined protocol.

Onboarding New Students and Families

We believe that effective communication with new students and families not only helps build relational trust with them but also provides an opportunity to gather information that will save teachers time and energy. Our school's community ambassador created a new student checklist that onboards new students and families in a warm and welcoming way and communicates relevant information to their teachers in a timely fashion—without requiring teachers to spend additional time after school trying to gather this information.

When a new student is assigned after the school year starts, our community ambassador reaches out and sets up a meeting on the student's first day. When the family arrives, they are greeted with a smile, given a goody bag full of school supplies and school swag, given a tour of the school, and have a meeting to review paperwork and share important information about the student and family. Figure 3.4 is a copy of the plan we use (created by our community ambassador, Carren Cook).

FIGURE 3.4
New Student Plan Checklist

New Student Plan Checklist

Steps for the Ambassador

Student Name: _____ Student Phone #: _____

Parent/Guardian Name: _____

Emergency Contact: _____

Assigned Teacher: _____

Transportation: _____

Lunch #: _____

	Ambassador greets and welcomes students and family to school. Escorts to the community room.
	Verifies language and obtains interpreter if needed.
	Student provided with ☐ lanyard ☐ supply bag ☐ memento ☐ Chromebook
	Ambassador escorts the student (and family) to the classroom where they are greeted by the teacher.
	Family meets with the ambassador to confirm transportation home and emergency contact. Ambassador conducts a family interview. *Note: If a family is unable to stay due to time commitment, the ambassador schedules a Google Meet to conduct the interview, as well as connecting them with Dojo, Parent Place, Portal, etc.*
	Family is gifted with a school yard sign or door hanger.
	Ambassador ensures cafeteria is informed, obtains a lunch number, and assigns a seat number for student.
	Prior to dismissal, ambassador confirms transportation home with the teacher and ensures a student buddy will accompany the new student to the bus or car rider room.
	Ambassador checks in with family that evening and again weekly for the first month.
	Note: If student is in grades 3–5, ambassador assists student in choosing a Friday club.

Communicating About Your School

How are you using social media to communicate with families and community members about the great things going on in your school? Are you the school's chief storyteller, crafting the narrative you want everyone to know about all the amazing things your staff is doing? Or are you letting all those magical moments go unnoticed? The use of social media can help combat the negative narrative that exists around teaching and education as a whole. When you share what you are doing, it also adds to the larger professional network of teaching and learning. What better way to lift the morale of a teacher, team, or building than to highlight the great things going on in your school's classrooms for the world to see.

Establishing systems that provide clear and consistent forms of communication will help support a culture of transparency, clarity, and trust. In addition to a reduced sense of frustration, teachers will feel supported and will appreciate the way you demonstrate the value of their time and input. By fostering open dialogue, empathy, and collaboration, you create an environment in which the collective wisdom and expertise of both teachers and administrators can flourish and avoid contributing to a sense of burnout.

Think-Abouts

1. Does your school have a living calendar or hub where all important communication is easily accessible? If so, how has the protocol for its use been communicated to staff? If not, what is a realistic goal to launch this for your staff?
2. How do you ensure that your weekly communication embeds a balance of information, celebration, encouragement, and opportunity for growth?
3. When reflecting on your meeting structure and schedule, how do you ensure that all meetings are necessary?

4. How have you organized your meetings in a way that helps stream-line communication?

5. How are your forms of communication organized? Do all staff have equitable access?

6. What systems do you have in place to onboard and communicate with new staff members?

7. How are you using social media to communicate the great things your school is doing and combat the negative narrative that exists around teacher burnout?

PART II

Systems and Structures
That Support the
Whole Teacher

4

Support Inside the Classroom

"You have to have a culture that embraces, supports, and is committed to these students and their success. Once you have that platform, then you can start to think about programs."

—Kim Wilcox

🔋 Burnout Challenge

Teachers feel frustrated by an increase in student misbehavior, which prevents them from being able to teach. The increase in trauma needs that emerged in the wake of the COVID-19 pandemic has required teachers to devote more time to dealing with social-emotional needs than academic content. This, coupled with the pressure of high-stakes accountability and a need to combat learning loss, has increased the complexity and challenge of making sure students are transition ready. Inconsistent or ineffective administrative support for student behavior and discipline, combined with the increased mental health needs of students, can leave teachers feeling underresourced, unsupported, and unsafe.

Ms. Wilson was in her ninth year teaching at the same school. In that time, she rarely wrote a referral and prided herself on "handling her own business" inside the classroom. In fact, she was often asked to mentor other teachers, and her colleagues routinely observed her class to learn different strategies for supporting classroom management. In the wake of the pandemic and online instruction, Ms. Wilson noticed an increase in student trauma, and it seemed as though the strategies that used to be successful no longer had the same impact. She found herself writing more referrals than in previous years and was going home exhausted every day.

In response to an increase in both internalizing (e.g., withdrawal, anxiety, sadness) and externalizing (e.g., stealing, cheating, aggression) behaviors many of her students were displaying, Ms. Wilson struggled to find an approach that worked, especially for one of her more challenging students, Elliot. Elliot had been a student at her school for three years, and although he had received referrals in the past, he was never considered one of the school's behavioral "highflyers." Early in the year, Elliot's disruptive behaviors were mostly limited to things like making noises, getting out of his seat and roaming the classroom, and calling out. Ms. Wilson used strategies such as proximity, planned ignoring, and recognizing and reinforcing positive behaviors. Initially, those strategies resulted in some success; however, the effect lessened over time, the disruptive behaviors increased, and Ms. Wilson's "bag of tricks" was soon running low. She called home frequently and—when she could reach Elliot's mom—was assured that Elliot's behavior would improve.

Unfortunately, things continued to get worse. Eventually, Ms. Wilson felt as if she spent all her time dealing with Elliot, which kept her from being able to teach the rest of the class. Feeling frustrated and overwhelmed, she began writing referrals in the hope that her principal and assistant principal would recognize how challenging things had gotten and provide her with appropriate support. Ms. Wilson realized, however, that instead of improving the situation with Elliot, the referrals made things worse and left her feeling frustrated and hopeless. Elliot would often be back in class within just a few minutes, and one time, he even returned with a piece of candy the assistant principal had given him! On top of everything, there was little to no communication or follow-up with her.

One day, Ms. Wilson arrived late to a team meeting and was in tears. When asked what was wrong, she replied, "I can't do this anymore. Student trauma needs are just too much, and the administration isn't doing anything about it. I go home exhausted each day and dread coming to work. I just want to teach, but because of the lack of support for discipline, I feel like all I do is put out fires."

One of the primary reasons teachers are leaving the profession is because they, like Ms. Wilson, don't feel supported in the classroom when it comes to student discipline (Long, 2010). As experienced school leaders, we know classroom management is one of the top areas of growth for new teachers. If left unsupported, classroom behavior can become a real problem, creating challenges for both the teacher and students, and consume the role of the administrator(s) who takes care of discipline.

In cases like Ms. Wilson's, student behavior isn't just one thing on a teacher's plate; it consumes the entire plate, leaving little if any room for anything else. Therefore, our next tip for reducing teacher burnout is providing support inside the classroom. Over the years, we have found the best way to support reactive behaviors is to put proactive supports in place. The ideas presented in this chapter are some of the tried-and-true strategies we use to support teachers and students inside the classroom. They have also led to a reduction in referrals and suspensions and have enhanced our overall school culture, resulting in our school becoming the only school in the state of Kentucky (at the time of writing) to be named a National School of Character.

Emotional Well-Being First, Content Second

The external pressure to address learning loss and close achievement gaps sometimes forces teachers to feel as though they must jump into academic content on the first day of school in order to "cover" everything. If you are going to successfully establish a culture of proactive support, then it is essential to anchor your collective commitments in activities that reflect that. An intense schoolwide focus on building relationships and establishing daily routines through intentional community-building activities with students during the first three weeks of school is nonnegotiable.

Although some teachers may be anxious to scrap the "fluff" and jump straight into content, it is essential that you—as the leader—set expectations for prioritizing community and a sense of belonging with students. Having "permission" from you to intentionally design lessons that are focused on social and emotional well-being will reduce teachers' anxiety and create an investment in positive student behavior that will reap benefits throughout the year.

The timeline to teach content can be fairly tight, but we have to keep in mind that there are some days students simply cannot learn or retain content because they are so emotionally unstable. Therefore, structures must be put in place to ensure social-emotional learning (SEL) is an embedded part of the day. This does not mean teachers scrap content altogether or sit back and don't teach for an entire day. Instead, look for ways SEL can be naturally integrated into the daily schedule. One way to do this and provide intentional support at the beginning of each day is a morning meeting (Woolf, n.d.). The purpose of a morning meeting is to create a safe and inclusive environment that ensures everyone feels seen and heard. This can be done with an individual greeting, ensuring students understand their schedule and structure for the day, and an activity to help the class connect over a common question or topic. Incorporating "brain breaks"—activities that incorporate movement and mindfulness— throughout the day is another way to support whole-class needs.

When approached with intentionality, whole-class SEL strategies and activities provide support for most students in a class. Students with increased trauma may need more support and should receive daily check-ins with a trusted adult. Every student should have at least one trusted adult in the building with whom they can talk. To achieve this goal, we are intentional with the way we structure morning supervisory duty and ensure that every student who enters the building passes at least three adults who greet them before they even get to their classroom. As school leaders (principal and counselor), we position ourselves in a location that allows all students to access us when they arrive. Our physical presence not only makes us available to greet and troubleshoot student needs before they get to the classroom but also provides a model for visible leadership. Visible leadership cannot be understated. When staff members observe us in the hallway greeting students, it acts as a model for positive interaction and helps build mutual respect—because we're not asking them to do anything we aren't willing to or don't do ourselves.

Students at our school are also greeted by name when they enter their homeroom. This may seem like a small thing, but when a teacher isn't standing at the classroom door, it can be the difference between a successful or unsuccessful day for a student. Therefore, as the leader, you must set expectations for your teachers and monitor implementation. What you expect and inspect is what they will respect.

Beyond the classroom, we also have a behavior support team composed of the school counselor, mental health practitioner, and behavior coach. This team supports students with more significant ongoing needs and offers movement breaks, small-group instruction, and one-on-one support to address student needs throughout the day.

Providing a comprehensive system of supports for social-emotional needs means focusing on both your students and your teachers. Let's face it: sometimes a teacher needs a break because they are triggered by a student or a student's behavior. It's therefore important to create a system with a behavior support team that provides class coverage if and when a teacher needs to step away. As the leader, it is also important that you help your teachers identify those triggers so they know when to ask for help. In your career, you've likely dealt with a student who knows exactly how to push your buttons. As humans, we need to take a break every now and then to continue being our best selves—instead of responding in a way that breaks the trust of the students and staff around us. Teaching teachers how to do just that not only helps in the moment but also helps you identify further ways to support those teachers over the course of the school year.

Finally, it is critical that you develop a plan for how you will intentionally and proactively utilize your counselors and mental health support personnel. We have a structure to support all classrooms on a weekly, biweekly, or monthly basis, depending on social-emotional data. During the summer, our administrative team meets to review end-of-year behavior data to establish preliminary behavior interventions for the beginning of the next school year to help ease the transition from one year to the next. Having a system that implements proactive supports focused on emotional well-being before diving into content helps reduce reactive responses to behavior.

Push-In Versus Pull-Out Support

When students are struggling and teachers need reactive support, certain students really enjoy leaving the classroom to escape or avoid the task at hand (Chazin et al., 2021). Removing a student from a classroom may provide immediate relief for the teacher, but it also reinforces the student's desire to escape or avoid and often leads to more disruptive behaviors in the long run. Noticing this trend, we made a shift in our practices to implement more of a push-in model (Sailor et al., 2021), rather than a pull-out approach. Transitioning to a push-in model not only allows students to receive one-on-one support for behavior and mental health but also reduces their ability to escape or avoid their task. In turn, this helps reduce the number of disruptive behaviors teachers experience in the classroom.

This was a huge shift for us. Prior to making this transition, if a student were displaying inappropriate behaviors, the teacher would write a referral on a triplicate referral form provided by the district and send the offending student to the office with the referral. Depending on administrator availability, the situation might have been dealt with immediately or the student could have been left sitting in the front office for hours before being addressed. We also didn't have a designated protocol for "dealing with" situations, which resulted in inconsistent consequences for students and communication with teachers. Frustration and dissatisfaction with these inconsistencies were a staple of the after-school parking lot chatter and highlighted in our statewide working conditions survey.

Let's face it: If you're an administrator responding to disruptive behavior in the classroom, you likely have at least a dozen other tasks happening simultaneously. It is much easier to pull the student out of the classroom so you can continue to do your work at the same time. However, what happens over time is that you create the need for this response because the student will continue those behaviors (likely more frequently) because they are getting exactly what they want. However, if you take time on the front end and push in to support when you first start noticing this trend, it will save you a lot of time later on.

If teachers are accustomed to having students removed every time they write a referral, then the push-in model will likely be a transition for them as well. They may not understand why the misbehaving student remains in their class; therefore, it is important that you provide insight into the rationale behind keeping the student in class. Remember, students can't learn if they aren't in class. It should be noted that even when you adopt a push-in model for behavior support, there will be incidents in which students will need to be removed for safety reasons. Identifying which behaviors warrant push-in support versus those that require pull-out support will be discussed later in this chapter.

MTSS for Proactive Behavior Supports

A multitiered system of supports (MTSS) is a process to help school staff analyze data through a schoolwide sustainable model (Sailor et al., 2021). Although many schools are adept at the MTSS approach they take to implementing proactive interventions for academic support, they often neglect to apply the same principles to behavior. Having an MTSS that tightly aligns both behavior and academics will create support systems that lead to optimal success for both students and teachers.

Our approach is to meet biweekly and discuss individual student data and schoolwide trends. The team is composed of our principal, assistant principal, school counselor, academic coach, special education implementation coach, mental health practitioner, and behavior coach. We also have an outside organization that provides school-based therapy and attends occasionally to discuss students they serve. This team is responsible for accepting referrals from teachers for students they feel need one-on-one or small-group support. The team is also responsible for monitoring the interventions put in place for each of these students and for discussing progress based on referral data, observations, and teacher reports.

The year before we began holding regular MTSS meetings, we had the highest number of suspensions in a decade. Recognizing that something needed to change, we began to implement this MTSS protocol for behavior, modeling our approach on how we met to discuss MTSS academics. The first year we took this streamlined approach, our suspensions decreased by 70 percent. There is no doubt that the process had a major impact on our proactive and reactive interventions for support.

To ensure that no student is overlooked, each homeroom teacher should complete a universal screener for behavior. We use the student risk screening scale (SRSS; Lane & Menzies, 2009). This screener is a great tool because it breaks down internalizing and externalizing behaviors and tiers each of them accordingly. Like MTSS for academics, tiers are used to indicate the level of support each student needs to be successful. Tier 1 behavior support is the universal support or core SEL curriculum that is provided to all students through the schoolwide behavior support plan. Tier 2 indicates that a student needs additional support, such as small-group counseling or a social-skills group a few times each week. Tier 3 indicates that a student needs daily, one-on-one intensive support, which could include social-skills instruction with a counselor or behavior coach combined with mental health support from a specialized practitioner or outside therapeutic agency. The cells within the SRSS spreadsheet that we use are designed to change colors based on a student's overall score to indicate if they need Tier 2 or 3 supports. If a cell changes to yellow, it indicates a need for Tier 2 support, whereas a red cell indicates a need for Tier 3 support. Therefore, the subjectivity of the tiering system is removed when using the color coding on the spreadsheet. Conducting an SRSS analysis three times a year helps ensure that all students who are in need of additional support receive it.

In addition to helping identify all students who need additional support, the SRSS screener also helps the MTSS team decide the level of support each classroom needs. Based on the data from the screener, decisions can be made about differentiated levels of whole-class support. Depending on the percentage of internalizing and externalizing behaviors observed, a classroom may be assigned to weekly, biweekly, or monthly counseling. Using this data helps make the decision objective and gives intentionality to counseling services.

After the data is analyzed, a support plan and schedule can be created to ensure all tier 2 and tier 3 students receive appropriate interventions, based on their identified needs. Like MTSS for academics, the team makes decisions about the intervention, frequency, goals, and progress monitoring tools that will be used for each student. At the end of each response to intervention (RTI) cycle, the team meets to analyze student progress toward established goals and adjust their plans as necessary.

The SRSS data allow us to take a comprehensive look at the school-wide needs for individual classrooms and students, but one of the ways we have most successfully used these data is to inform our school counseling program. Our first year back to in-person instruction, postpandemic, was an incredibly challenging social-emotional time for students. When our teachers completed the SRSS in the fall, there were certain classrooms that had 65 percent of students identified as needing tier 2 or tier 3 support for internalizing needs, externalizing behaviors, or both. Therefore, we had to place a heavy focus on tier 1 instruction for 11 of our classes. To meet this need, we set up weekly classroom counseling lessons with seven of those classrooms and biweekly lessons with the other four (based on the number of students who needed support). The remaining 13 classes in our school stayed on a monthly counseling rotation. This allowed the counseling lessons to be intentional and targeted to the needs of each class.

Of particular interest within these data were the number of students struggling with internalizing and externalizing behaviors in our 4th grade classrooms. As an administrative team, we were already aware of the externalizing behavioral needs in that grade, but the number of students exhibiting internalizing behaviors helped us understand why compassion fatigue had set in so early in the school year with those particular teachers. They were supporting students emotionally on such a deep level that it took a toll much earlier than it would during a "typical" school year. We realized that we needed to give extra support to those teachers. Providing tier 1 counseling instruction was a great way to start because that time allowed them to have a break within the school day. We also provided one-on-one time with the teacher and a counselor during individualized professional development (IPD) days. Through all of this, teachers were able to get tier 1 support for their students, a break to step away for a few minutes, time to regroup during the week, and time to process the school year with the counselor every six weeks. As a result of this implementation and approach, six students moved back to tier 1 for internalizing and externalizing by spring of the same school year.

Racial Equity, Culturally Responsive, and Trauma Training

More than ever, it's imperative for staff to receive intentional and ongoing racial equity and culturally responsive training. So as not to overwhelm teachers or make it feel like "one more thing" on their teachers' plate, create a schedule that embeds training throughout your professional learning communities (PLCs), professional development days, and/or faculty meetings. Having a year-at-a-glance plan will not only allow you to stay intentional and focused with your equity work but also allow your staff to see how it is embedded throughout all your systems.

Our PLC work includes several different components. First, we use a district-developed tool to ensure our lessons are culturally inclusive before we teach them. We also ensure that all grade levels partner with a multilingual learner specialist to establish language goals, objectives, considerations, and scaffolds for multilingual learners prior to the instruction. Both of these offer ways for teachers to think through an asset-based lens about culture, language, and equity prior to teaching content. Making these cultural considerations is specifically important when planning for student behavior purposes because culturally responsive teaching practices have a direct correlation with increased positive student behaviors (Larson et al., 2018). As a result of our concentrated efforts to meet the diverse learning needs of all our students, our school was recognized as a National ESEA Distinguished School in 2021.

Beyond our PLCs, we have a team of teachers who comprise a racial equity committee and help drive the equity work in our building. The first activity this committee engaged in was a jigsaw book study in which members chose one of five books. This activity allowed us to start the work of our own social awareness and build capacity within that team. This work is far from finished, but it has helped propel us into the work we continue to do today—including monthly meetings to discuss takeaways from ongoing book studies and ideas for how we can apply our learning with the whole staff. Having a committee that includes representation from across the school helps build capacity both vertically and horizontally. When engaging in the work of diversity, equity, and inclusion, we recommend using the A4 model for cultural competence (see Figure 4.1; Kentucky Department of Education, 2022).

Another important consideration to keep in mind is training in trauma-responsive practices. This is a powerful addition because it helps reshape teachers' perceptions from "Why are you doing this?" to "What has happened to make you do this?" Though trauma work is an ongoing process, it is very helpful for all staff to start thinking about student behavior through this lens. It helps take away the feeling of "failing to connect" with students and instead places an emphasis on the carryover students have from other situations—and the need for an outlet to release those feelings/emotions. How much teacher burnout in your building revolves around student behavior? Making this shift alone can be so powerful for your staff.

FIGURE 4.1
A4 Model for Cultural Competence

- **Awareness (A1)**
  – "Awareness of Self": What are my values, beliefs, norms, customs, traditions, styles, biases, stereotypes, and behaviors? *Who am I?*
  – "Awareness of Others": What are others' values, beliefs, norms, customs, traditions, styles, biases, stereotypes, and behaviors?

- **Acknowledgement (A2)**
  – How are my values, beliefs, norms, customs, traditions, styles, biases, stereotypes, and behaviors the same or different than others? *How am I?*

- **Acceptance (A3)**
  – Am I open to accepting and respecting differences? Why or why not? What are the benefits for me? What are the challenges for me?
  – Can I avoid assigning judgements (e.g., better/worse, right/wrong) to cultural differences? Why or why not?

- **Action (A4)**
  – What adjustments, both in the way I think and behave, do I need to make in order to effectively operate in a different cultural context?

Source: From Kentucky Department of Education (2022). www.education.ky.gov/teachers/Pages/A4-Modules.aspx

Schoolwide Behavior Support Plan

Inconsistencies in how administrators handle student behaviors, combined with lack of follow-through and follow-up, are the primary reasons teachers are leaving the profession (Walker, 2022). To help mitigate teacher frustration and provide an equitable approach to supporting students, a schoolwide behavior support plan that is developed collaboratively and shared with all stakeholders is a nonnegotiable for school leaders. Even though most people refer to behavior support plans as "discipline plans," we feel this term has a punitive connotation, whereas "schoolwide behavior support plans" refer to proactive and reactive strategies.

Many schoolwide behavior support plans focus almost exclusively on the *reactive* strategies administrators take when students display inappropriate behaviors. Although it is necessary to establish clear guidelines for consequences to help ensure consistency, neglecting to include *proactive* support as part of the plan will perpetuate a culture of punitive reaction. To that end, the rest of this chapter highlights the proactive approach outlined in our schoolwide behavior support plan.

We take a positive behavioral interventions and supports (PBIS) approach to supporting student behavior (Center on PBIS, 2022). The schoolwide behavior support plan we create as an administrative team, and revise each school year as necessary, reflects all the information presented earlier in this chapter. After all, it is important to ensure your systems and structures match what you say you are about and are consistently updated as your needs and understanding change. Figure 4.2 outlines the specific student behaviors in each tier of our behavior support plan to ensure all staff have a common understanding when approaching student support. The percentages reflect the defined ranges of the Center on PBIS (2022) tiered interventions.

The goal of any behavior support plan should be grounded in student and staff safety. As a way to prioritize safety, one of the most important pieces of our schoolwide behavior support plan is that all staff members have a walkie-talkie and are able to reach us for any type of need (e.g., student-requested break, classroom support, medical emergency). This ensures all teachers have access to support exactly when they need it, regardless of the reason. Our administrative and behavioral support team members have a specific channel, and our housekeeping staff and front office staff both have dedicated channels. Having all necessary parties available for immediate support helps ensure open lines of communication for different needs.

FIGURE 4.2

Tiered Approach to Supporting Behavior

Tier	Examples of Behaviors	Approaches to Support Behaviors	Percentage of Students Who Exhibit These Behaviors
Tier 1	• Is off task • Talks out of turn • Doesn't follow directions • Moves out of area	• Nonverbal prompts and cues • Reminders of expectations • Review classroom expectations • Private conferencing	80%+
Tier 2	• Yells out continuously • Puts hands on others • Refuses to participate/work • Frequently makes fun of others • Gets out of seat frequently without permission • Cries inconsolably • Rolls on the floor • Climbs inside lockers	• All tier 1 supports • Verbal prompts and cues • Redirection • Breaks (option for inside and outside the classroom) • Visual supports (timer, boundary, etc.)	10 to 15%
Tier 3	• Endangers self or others • Impedes the learning of others • Fights • Brings a weapon to school	• All tier 1 and 2 supports • Call for administrative support	1 to 5%

In addition, we created a code system so when a teacher needs support, they use a specific code (e.g., admin is code 1) whenever they need someone to respond to help a student in their classroom. For example, a teacher may call in a "code 3," which means they need a specific team to come quickly (for a fight or when a particular behavior has escalated, placing the rest of the class in potential danger). The code system helps us know who needs to respond and the urgency of the situation. It is also essential to have a hierarchy of who responds when only one person is needed. This helps limit the lag time in response since we know no one is ever just sitting around waiting to be called.

The final key component of any schoolwide behavior support plan should be the follow-up after an incident when a teacher calls for support. When teachers don't receive any follow-up communication, their frustration only intensifies, and the experience can leave them feeling distrustful of the entire plan. Skipping this essential step can also lead to teachers feeling as though "nothing was done" to support them when they called for assistance. A common form of follow-up communication (email, Google form, handwritten form) should be established and utilized by the entire administrative team. It is a good idea to practice completing the follow-up communication as a team to calibrate a common understanding.

There also needs to be a follow-up with the student by a member of the mental health support team to process the behaviors that occurred in the classroom. This can include a reflection of the incident and the behaviors exhibited along with teaching (or reteaching) replacement behaviors should a similar situation arise in the future.

Consistency Across the Administrative Team

No behavior support plan can be successful without communication and consistency. One approach for consistency is to ensure that all response team members are part of the MTSS behavior support meetings. During those meetings, the team should analyze individual student data and calibrate the response to behaviors so that no matter who responds to the classroom, everyone is on the same page about what the student needs. For example, if a student just needs to go for a walk to gather their thoughts and calm down, then everyone on the team needs to know that so they respond in the same way. By contrast, if another student has a history of escaping to avoid work and wants to leave the classroom to fulfill that need, then all team members need to know that as well—so they can keep that student in the classroom if they respond.

Calibration and consistency are necessary not only for the student—so they know what to expect—but also for the teacher. Teachers need to know what to expect from you when you respond so it creates less of a disruption for them and the other students in the classroom. When two team members respond differently, it gives off the appearance of a lack of communication, which in turn breeds mistrust.

To help provide feedback to schools about teacher satisfaction with their working conditions, our state administers a survey every two years. Part of that survey focuses on managing student conduct and asks staff to rate their level of agreement with the following statements:

- Students at this school understand expectations for their conduct.
- Students at this school follow rules of conduct.
- Policies and procedures about student conduct are clearly understood by the faculty.
- School administrators consistently enforce rules for student conduct.
- School administrators support teachers' efforts to maintain discipline in the classroom.
- Teachers consistently enforce rules for student conduct.
- The faculty work in a school environment that is safe.

Prior to implementing our schoolwide behavior support plan, our results in the behavior support category were less than satisfactory and indicated an average agreement rate in the 70s (meaning only 70 percent of the staff agreed with the statements). After the implementation, however, the average agreement rate increased to the 90s. When reviewing the plan with staff at the beginning of the year, and when meeting with teachers during coaching sessions, we reference these questions to determine if our teachers feel supported, which guides our ongoing administrative decision making around behavioral support.

Analyzing Data to Identify Trends

Earlier, we discussed data analysis as a core component of MTSS behavior team meetings. Essential data points for analysis should include individual student referral data, classroom referral data, and schoolwide data broken down by race, gender, grade, location, and time. Although no two MTSS meetings will look the same, there are actions you can take to maximize the team's time to reach its goals. In advance, the chair of the team should create and distribute an agenda that outlines assigned roles and responsibilities and identifies the data point(s) you will analyze. This ensures everyone comes to the meeting prepared.

A primary source of the data we analyze is captured in a shared online document (see Figure 4.3). When teachers call a code, they complete the form to help the team better understand the antecedents, behaviors, and consequences. This helps identify trends or patterns in the data. Do the incidents happen at the same time of day? With a particular teacher? In a particular part of the building? Sometimes there are no patterns at all; that's also helpful to know. The form allows us to analyze the function of the student's behavior (e.g., to avoid a task or to gain attention) so we can better tailor the support plan and target the student's precise needs.

Collecting and analyzing this information is important to help all students with social-emotional needs. However, it is critical for students who exhibit more significant needs. We once had a student we'll call Neveah (not her real name). Neveah struggled to interact with peers and adults. When we discussed her as a team, it felt as if she were unsuccessful in almost every content area. She struggled everywhere! We also felt like we had tried everything and would constantly spin our wheels whenever we had a pop-up meeting with intervention specialists or her classroom teacher.

At an MTSS meeting, our team sat down to look at Neveah's data to see the specifics of her day. To our surprise, we realized that she was almost always successful in math, which led us to ask the following questions: *What is it about math that makes her successful? Are there different adults or teachers who support her during that time? Is there anything we could transfer from that class/experience to make her successful in other areas?*

FIGURE 4.3
Sample Behavior Incident Log

Behavior Incident Log Form Questions

Incident Level:

1. Confined to student
2. Disrupts others in area
3. Disrupts everyone in class
4. Disrupts other classrooms or common area of school
5. Behavior causes or threatens to cause physical injury to student or others

Time _____

Date _____

Subject _____

Antecedent of the Behavior _____

Type of Behavior _____

Response to the Behavior _____

Additional Comments/Notes _____

What we learned from this analysis is that there was a particular support staff member who really connected with Neveah during math time. With that in mind, we rearranged that staff member's schedule to provide more support to Neveah throughout the day. She was available during breaks in other content areas and for check-ins/check-outs during the school day. Increasing the amount of support and connection Neveah received from this particular person significantly reduced the number of referrals—by about 50 percent—within the first month of implementation. Utilizing data from the online form helped us identify the specific time she was successful, which helped us better understand the specific support she needed to be successful throughout the day.

Before using this form, teachers were completing this same information on a paper form. This meant they had to keep up with the paper copies and turn them in to the administrative team, who would then have to graph the data in order to see trends across the building and by student. Using an online form has reduced the burden associated with all those steps. Google Forms, for example, will graph the data for you. Now, when we meet as a team, it is easy to pull up the data and look at building trends—or just extract the data for one specific student to determine if interventions are working.

Hub for Resources

If you are like us and have multiple people who help respond to or support student behavior in your building, take a second to think about where they are located. In our case, we were spread out in different rooms around the building. As we became more intentional about our support, we decided to create a mental health hub. This meant that we all moved into offices or rooms close to one another in an effort to share resources, fidgets, and other sensory strategies throughout the day. (Some of our favorites include textured seat cushions, alternative seating options such as standing desks and wobble chairs, chew items for sensory processing, Theraputty, and stress balls.) It also gave us an opportunity to do quick check-ins with one another if a particular student was really struggling that day. Your building may require two or three hubs, depending on its size. Regardless, think about the "hot spots" in your building, the resources and staff you currently have, and how you could intentionally situate them throughout the building to best serve your population.

Recall Ms. Wilson from the beginning of this chapter. Fortunately, her team leaders shared their frustrations with the principal. With a desire to make sure his teachers felt supported, the principal met with Ms. Wilson to acknowledge her concerns and discuss a plan for making sure she, and all teachers in the school, felt supported inside the classroom. He then met with his administrative support team to develop a schoolwide behavior support plan, which provided proactive support and consistency across the administrative staff. The school counselor started meeting with Elliot to provide SEL interventions and with his mother to create a plan for wraparound support at home. As a result, behavior referrals decreased, engagement increased, and teacher satisfaction improved.

This chapter is full of the strategies we use to support student behavior. We spent a great deal of time going through these systems and structures because we know that behavior can be one of the biggest factors in teacher burnout. With intentional proactive supports and a clear plan, you can mitigate some of the behaviors that lead to teacher burnout before they even start. Having a comprehensive behavior support plan that is grounded in proactive support and driven by data analysis will help make your job easier and more enjoyable. In addition, you will be able to spend less time as a manager putting out fires and more time as an instructional leader focusing on improving student achievement.

Think-Abouts

1. How have you ensured that you have an effective MTSS for behavior that supports a proactive, rather than a reactive, approach? Can you develop a plan to push in rather than pull students out of the classroom?

2. How can you truly involve stakeholders in developing a schoolwide behavior plan that clearly identifies behaviors in all three tiers and has a clear process for referring students?

3. How do you ensure consistency among your administrative team as it relates to understanding and implementing the schoolwide behavior support plan?

4. Do you have a clearly defined communication plan for follow-up when a behavioral incident occurs? If not, how could you incorporate this to make it sustainable over the long term?

5. How do you ensure that your MTSS meetings occur on a regular basis?

6. How does your team analyze behavior data to see if your interventions are working? Is this done on a regular basis?

7. How have you or how could you discuss cultural implications within your behavior data?

5

Coaching and Feedback

"Coaching is unlocking a person's potential to maximize their growth."

—John Whitmore

> **▢▢▢ Burnout Challenge**
>
> Teachers are expected to provide feedback and support to students but often feel as though the feedback and support they receive from administration is inconsistent, ineffective, or nonexistent. Lack of coaching time with the administrative team can leave teachers feeling neglected, isolated, and unsupported.

Ms. Rodriguez, 3rd grade teacher at Travel Elementary, found herself growing increasingly frustrated. Despite her best efforts to excel in her profession, she yearned for guidance, coaching, and meaningful feedback from her administrator. The absence of support left her feeling adrift and uncertain of her progress, yet eager to unlock her full potential.

One afternoon, as Ms. Rodriguez sat in her classroom, she reflected on her journey as an educator. She knew that feedback and coaching were crucial components for professional growth and development. Attempting to mitigate her frustration, she approached her administrator, Ms. Bolton, with a sincere and respectful request for more guidance and feedback. She expressed her desire for professional growth and highlighted her eagerness to receive constructive input that would help her refine her teaching practices. To her disappointment, Ms. Bolton seemed preoccupied and dismissive of Ms. Rodriguez's concerns. She assured Ms. Rodriguez that her performance was satisfactory but failed to offer any specific suggestions or support.

Ms. Rodriguez's experience highlights the frustration and longing that can arise when teachers lack coaching and feedback from their administrators. It also reminds us of the importance of nurturing teachers' professional growth through meaningful feedback and coaching, which ultimately benefits the entire school community. Though it is important for leaders to attract high-quality teachers, it is equally important that we focus on supporting and retaining the great teachers we already have. Failure to provide coaching, feedback, and professional development to support, enhance, and encourage teachers will lead to a diminished sense of capacity and job satisfaction, causing high-quality teachers to join the Great Resignation (Bryant et al., 2023).

In addition to an increased level of compassion fatigue that results from the secondary trauma teachers experience, increased demands associated with postpandemic schooling is creating an even greater level of burnout (Oberg et al., 2023). We expect a lot from our teachers, and, in return, we must intentionally give a lot to them. According to feedback from our staff, time and individualized support are the greatest gifts we can give them. Therefore, we created a system for coaching, feedback, and individualized professional development that supports teachers both professionally and personally. This system helped streamline each teacher's work in a clear direction, reducing unnecessary tasks that could otherwise pile on their plate. This chapter highlights that system and provides ideas for ways in which you can differentiate your approach with your teachers to help them not only improve their capabilities, performance, and well-being but also renew and invigorate their passion for teaching and learning.

Individualized Professional Development Protocol

Self-determination theory suggests that our growth and development needs are guided by three basic psychological needs: autonomy, competence, and relatedness (Ryan & Deci, 2000). When leaders create an environment for support and development that focuses on these three needs, coaching can significantly affect teacher success and well-being (Campbell & van Nieuwerburgh, 2018). Understanding the need to support our teachers both personally and professionally, we created a structure we refer to as individualized professional development (IPD) days. This structure allows us as leaders to provide equitable opportunities for our entire staff while differentiating the level and type of support they need. IPD days provide staff with one-on-one coaching, adult counseling, peer observation time, and individualized professional development. In addition to the other collaborative opportunities mentioned in Chapter 2, our teachers are provided with an opportunity for an IPD day once every six weeks. Figure 5.1 outlines the structure of IPD.

Having a coaching session with each teacher every six weeks is such a powerful move. Over the years, we've tried a variety of techniques to capture the content of coaching sessions but always ended up shuffling through various folders and paperwork instead of being able to devote full attention to the teachers in the sessions. Two years ago, we started using a teacher backpack, which is a digital portfolio created for each teacher. This digital backpack provides a hub to maintain important items, such as their beginning-of-the-year letter, classroom management plan, professional growth plan, feedback loop data, assessment results, and reflections. The teacher backpack also includes the following for review: class attendance percentages by month, teacher attendance by month, behavior codes called per month, family engagement data, MAP growth percentages, and coaching notes from each session.

Moving everything to a digital platform has been one of the best decisions we've ever made when it comes to coaching. It captures everything in one spot. Gone are the days of the five-inch binder portfolio to look through and the file cabinet full of observation notes. The teacher, principal, and assistant principal all have access to add documents. The other benefit of a digital teacher backpack is that it helps teachers stay organized from year to year, allowing them to consistently reflect and improve on previous years' work.

One-on-One Meetings and Professional Growth Plan

At the beginning of every year, we schedule one-on-one meetings with all staff members to set the tone for the year. Prior to this meeting, each staff member reviews their goals from the previous school year, various forms of data, and any other relevant documents to inform their ideas about where they want to focus their professional growth for the year. The meeting serves as a great opportunity not only to set expectations (on both sides) but also to ensure we clearly communicate schoolwide goals. Teachers engage in self-reflection by discussing their personal goals for growth and how reaching those goals will positively contribute to the overarching schoolwide goals.

Next, we help teachers develop SMART goals that include whole-class objectives and an equity-focused goal (Doran, 1981). In our district, we administer the MAP growth assessment and our teachers utilize it to develop their own growth goals. In the past, they've focused on proficiency percentages, and even though helping all students achieve proficiency is still a goal for our school, we have found that focusing on expected growth for each student is a more equitable measure. Teachers set goals around the percentage of their class that will meet their fall to spring growth goal.

In addition, they choose at least one subgroup that is underperforming and set an accelerated growth goal for that group. This equity-focused goal guides staff to be intentional with culturally responsive practices

FIGURE 5.1
Individualized Professional Development (IPD) Structure

Self-Reflection	
Purpose: To analyze strengths and priority areas of focus for growth	
What Teacher Is Doing	What Students Are Doing
Reviewing data and any other relevant content documents to complete a self-reflection	N/A

One-on-One Meeting	
Purpose: To analyze strengths and priority areas of focus for growth	
What Teacher Is Doing	What Students Are Doing
Meeting with principal and assistant principal to discuss self-assessment and professional growth plans for the year as well as support and resources needed	Engaging in additional special-area time

Professional Growth Plan	
Purpose: To document professional growth goals and plan	
What Teacher Is Doing	What Students Are Doing
Utilizing self-reflection and one-on-one meeting to determine plans for professional growth goal(s). Documenting growth goal on PGP form and uploading to teacher backpack folder	N/A

Feedback Loop Visits	
Purpose: To celebrate and provide feedback; coaching team will visit classrooms to celebrate and provide individualized feedback	
What Teacher Is Doing	What Students Are Doing
Implementing all the great strategies they have to engage students	Engaging and learning at high levels

Coaching/Counseling Sessions	
Purpose: To provide feedback and support based on individual needs as outlined in PGP	
What Teacher Is Doing	What Students Are Doing
Meeting with principal and assistant principal to engage in coaching and feedback, then meeting with counselor for intentional ME time	Engaging in compassion/social justice lessons with CSP teacher in the classroom

Peer Observations	
Purpose: To learn from and provide feedback to peers based on peer observation norms	
What Teacher Is Doing	What Students Are Doing
Observing peers to gain ideas and give feedback	Engaging in additional special area or counseling

Individualized Professional Development	
Purpose: To provide feedback and support based on individualized needs as outlined in PGP	
What Teacher Is Doing	What Students Are Doing
Engaging in professional development that supports their individual growth plan. This can include the following: • Articles • Books • Blogs • Videos • Meetings with instructional coach • Other	Engaging in additional special area or counseling

Reflection	
Purpose: To reflect on learning and goals set for IPD	
What Teacher Is Doing	What Students Are Doing
Completing IPD reflection and uploading to teacher backpack folder	N/A

that accelerate learning and focus on closing gaps between subgroups. A spreadsheet is maintained with each teacher's goals and achieved data from year to year to help monitor progress and ensure they are selecting goals that are indeed SMART.

Finally, we ask teachers to identify strategies they will engage in to meet their goals and what professional development and resource needs they have. Teachers utilize the content from our beginning-of-the-year meeting to guide the development of their professional growth plan, and we do the same to focus future coaching and feedback.

Feedback Loop Visits

When your teachers hear the word *walkthrough,* what effect does it have on them? Do they get excited about the value it will add to their professional growth? Or do they cringe a little? Despite the valuable data walkthroughs can provide a school, the term *walkthrough* often has a very negative connotation with teachers. We have found this to be true when talking with leaders at all levels from across the country. The reasons can vary, but commonalities that often make walkthroughs unwelcome and unwanted include length (they're either too long or too short), a lack of training and calibration for those who conduct them, and a deficit focus on what's missing.

We've seen (and used) several walkthrough tools in our careers. Some have been suggested by colleagues, and some have been district requirements. Some have provided meaningful data, and some have increased frustration for us and our teachers. Although some tools were more successful than others, none of them was able to meet the differentiated needs of staff or help create a system that was sustainable over time.

We understand the power of providing feedback to students, so we wanted a system that could provide this same powerful practice for teachers. To that end, we dug deeper into various forms of walkthroughs, along with feedback tools and resources, and discovered why our walkthrough and feedback system never gained traction the way we had wanted it to.

First, we lacked clarity about the basic purpose of a walkthrough. We had assumed that all tools were seemingly created equal with the same universal purpose, despite the length or content focus. Some required in-depth written feedback, whereas others required a simple selection from a drop-down menu. The problem was that walkthroughs and informal observations plus feedback were being utilized interchangeably. It's true that they both gather information that can guide coaching conversations for teachers, but they can significantly vary in length, breadth, and frequency.

Walkthroughs are meant to provide snapshots of evidence over a series of short classroom visits. They should be focused and frequent, providing data that can help identify trends for individuals and groups. An example of an effective walkthrough tool we used was from *The Fundamental Five* (Laird & Cain, 2011). By using this walkthrough protocol, we were able to spend three to five minutes in every teacher's classroom multiple times per week to gather data about implementation of the high-quality practices outlined in Laird and Cain's work: framing the lesson, working in the power zone, frequent small-group purposeful talk, recognizing and reinforcing, and writing critically. We utilized these data to help guide instructional practices until every teacher was regularly engaging in these high-leverage practices.

Engaging in these practices was important for our teachers to influence student achievement, but we still wanted to provide them with longer, more detailed feedback that was focused on the areas of growth they had identified during our beginning-of-the-year meeting. To achieve this, we left notebooks in each room with the goal of visiting frequently and leaving feedback for them. At first, this seemed to be a hit. The teachers loved the feedback, and it created invaluable conversations about their instruction. Then, as the year continued and the additional demands of the job set in, it became increasingly difficult to visit every teacher's room multiple times a week and leave specific and descriptive feedback.

Unfortunately, frustration and discouragement on both sides increased because we had created an effective walkthrough system that simply wasn't sustainable. In essence, what we had established was a feedback cycle—not a walkthrough system. Recognizing the difference between the two provided much needed grace and guidance. Perhaps you have experienced similar challenges, or perhaps you have a highly effective system you use to gather walkthrough data and provide feedback to teachers. Regardless of where you fall on this continuum, I think we can all agree that attempting to conduct informal observations to provide descriptive feedback to teachers within the frequency expectations of a walkthrough should be avoided.

We spent several years trying a variety of tools and protocols, which produced mostly marginal coaching and feedback results, before we decided to implement feedback loop visits. The goal of these is to provide detailed and targeted feedback using individualized feedback forms based on teacher-identified goals. Our teachers find these to be meaningful and actually look forward to our visits! During our coaching sessions, we ask about something that is going well in their classroom (that they would like to celebrate) and something they would like specific feedback on (to advance their practice toward their professional growth goals). We then create an individualized document (on Google Forms) for each teacher that lists these celebration practices and feedback goals. We include the former as part of the feedback loop visit to acknowledge what is going well, and we provide the latter in the area(s) identified by the teacher. We also include a section for additional comments, which allows us to provide feedback about something the teacher didn't specifically request or call out. Our goal is to visit each teacher once or twice every two weeks and provide them with feedback that is timely, specific, and positive. (Save the areas for growth for coaching sessions.)

Here is an example:

Thank you for allowing me to be part of your Reader's Workshop today. Great job revisiting the lesson frame during your closure. This allowed students to stay focused and see the connection between your expectations written on the board and the "why" behind their work. Your students were all so engaged with their text! The share-time (closure) really holds students accountable, and the specific feedback you give each student will not only help them grow as learners, but it also models for other students the type of feedback to give. I also want to thank you for continuing to be so reflective in your practice. Keep up the great work!

Coaching Sessions

In many buildings, there is a negative coaching culture because coaching has been reserved for nonrenewed teachers and/or teachers in need of intensive support. We contend that, like every athlete, every teacher deserves a coach. Coaching provides individualized time for teachers to reflect on their practices, celebrate their progress toward their goals, and recalibrate pacing and needs. Effective coaching sessions are grounded in trusting relationships. Creating a culture in which teachers feel comfortable taking risks is nonnegotiable. If we expect teachers to be vulnerable and reflective, then we must create conditions that encourage and invite that. Therefore, our coaching protocol is separate from the evaluation cycle. The way we see it, coaching and feedback should be used formatively to guide improved practice for summative evaluations. As long as teachers feel like the goal of coaching and feedback is to gather evidence that may negatively affect their evaluation, they will remain guarded and less open to giving and receiving feedback.

It is important that we differentiate the coaching that takes place between teachers *and administrators* and the coaching that takes place between teachers *and instructional coaches*. For administrators, the goal should be to coach with a wide lens. Leaders should help teachers see the big picture and understand how they can support them. The role of the instructional coach, by contrast, should be to work alongside teachers and provide support through planning, modeling, and on-the-spot coaching to implement day-to-day practices. Therefore, it is critical for principals and other leaders to work closely with instructional coaches to reduce overlap and maintain momentum toward goals.

There are a variety of coaching models that exist, but we've found that there is not one model that fits the needs of all staff. The following is an outline we use to get the conversation started in our coaching sessions.

Reflect on the unit(s) you have taught prior to this coaching session. Share your data analysis and instructional implications. (Focus on the whole class and equity-focus group.)

- Discuss implementation and impact of acceleration, interventions, and extensions.
- Pacing check: Share your scope and sequence. Where are you? Are you on pace? Why or why not?
- How is your PLC going? What's your role?
- Share the new form and add the area of feedback the teacher would like specific feedback on.
- Where are you going for peer observations?
- What are you doing for IPD?
- Remember to reflect.

Teachers are given this outline (and any other data points they need to reference) before the coaching session. Teachers appreciate having the outline ahead of time because it allows them an opportunity to dig into their data and be more reflective during coaching sessions. In addition to the support and feedback they receive, teachers have also shared their appreciation for the accountability that coaching sessions provide.

At the end of each coaching session, we discuss what the teacher would like feedback on for the next six weeks, and we make this a point of intention as we conduct feedback loop visits. This allows us to differentiate our focus for each teacher and allows our feedback to be laser focused.

Counseling Sessions

This block of the IPD day is not "official" counseling. We refer to these blocks as counseling sessions because our counselor (Lara) provides this support for staff. The staff member responsible for this in your school is entirely up to you—and you can name this block however you feel is appropriate. However, to be successful, this should be a person most of your teachers trust and get along well with.

During these sessions, teachers should be able to get support with anything that may be affecting them in the classroom. For example, if a teacher is having trouble connecting with a particular student, this session could be focused on ways to build a stronger relationship or include extra support (e.g., additional observations and feedback, extra mental health support, breaks). The issue could also be personal in nature. For example, a teacher might be stressing out because of a difficulty getting their child to daycare and then to work on time. What we have found to be incredibly effective is just providing an opportunity for staff to vent if there is something stressful happening—along with a brainstorming session to identify ways we could potentially solve the issue. Whatever the situation, having an outlet to process and have someone listen—or even help problem solve—is such a game changer. It allows staff to feel like they are wholly supported, regardless of the issue.

Keep in mind that the most important aspect of this time is that the format is self-directed by staff. From taking a walk around the school to drawing or coloring, allowing staff to guide the direction of these "mental breaks" helps provide them with what they need personally. For most staff, this will become one of the most valued times of the year.

Peer Observations

Peer observations are cost-effective opportunities to help teachers work with one another in a mutually supportive way that builds a collegial culture (Campbell & van Nieuwerburgh, 2018). During this hour of their IPD day, teachers visit one another's classrooms to observe and gain insight into their colleagues' powerful practices. During coaching sessions, teachers are asked which classrooms they plan to visit during peer observation time. Sometimes they know where they want to visit, and sometimes they ask for recommendations based on what they hope to gain from the visit. This time provides mutual benefits by supporting growth goals for the visiting teacher and providing feedback for the host teacher. To establish clarity around purpose, it is important to develop peer observation norms. The norms we established are as follows:

- Follow the special-area schedule. (You can switch your individualized professional development and peer observation time if it better meets your needs.)
- Spend your time in classes that support your growth goals (i.e., "I am looking to focus on conferring in small groups, and Ms. Amazing does that well. I also want to see how Ms. Jones groups for centers and how Mr. Purple engages students in small-group purposeful talk).
- "Give some, take some" for each class you visit.
  - Give some: Using the feedback form, give feedback to the teacher you visited, based on their "feedback please focus" indicators and anything else you would like to celebrate.
  - Take one: Think about any takeaways you have for your own learning.
- Trust the process. Like anything new, we will work out the kinks as we go along.
- Maintain professionalism. This time is to be used for peer observations only (i.e., this is not time to meet with a parent, make copies, or do other administrative work).

Giving and receiving feedback are important elements of a growth-minded and reflective culture (van Nieuwerburgh, 2017). To help facilitate growth and minimize distractions, every teacher should have a folder that hangs in a mailbox outside their door. Within the folder is a form that identifies what they want feedback on, which may or may not be the same feedback they have requested from administrators during coaching time. Teachers also have blank copies of the feedback form they should complete and leave with the host teacher after peer observation time (Figure 5.2).

FIGURE 5.2
Peer Observation Feedback Form

Peer Observation Feedback		
Feedback for	Peer Observer	Date/Time

Feedback Please Focus Area:

Additional Feedback:

Think-Abouts:

Individualized Professional Development and Reflection

Cornett and Knight (2009) posit that traditional training methods do not lead to changes in classroom practice. One size does not fit all for students, and the same holds true for teachers. The need for whole-group professional development may still exist for items such as new curriculum implementation, but professional development must be differentiated to support the various needs of teachers.

One way we do this is by providing time within a teacher's IPD day for them to engage in personalized professional development that is catered to them both in content and delivery. During coaching sessions, teachers are expected to share what they will be doing during this time to further their own growth. Options can include book studies, articles, blogs, videos, and designated one-on-one time with the instructional coach. The primary goal is to ensure each teacher feels supported and resourced for their individual needs. At the end of an IPD day, teachers complete a reflection by responding to specific prompts:

- What is your professional growth focus?
- Discuss the professional learning you engaged in today, including your major takeaways.
- How will you apply this learning to your instructional practices?
- What needs do you have to support your next steps?

This reflection builds in a layer of accountability and provides insight about teachers' growth and additional needs. As with all reflections and paperwork that teachers are asked to submit, we recommend that you not only read all responses but also take time to respond to them. An important rule of thumb we follow is "If it is important enough to require the teacher to submit, then it is important enough for an administrator to provide feedback."

Coaching and Feedback Considerations

Providing feedback is one of the most significant ways a leader can influence teaching practices (Grissom et al., 2013). When establishing your systems and structures for coaching, feedback, and individualized professional development, make sure to consider the following:

- Culture of your building
- Needs of your building
- Experience level of your teachers
- Coaching experience of your admin team
- Written feedback (only focus on positives)
- Scheduling

Like you, we are always looking for ways to create more equitable practices for our staff and students. If you haven't yet checked out *Coaching for Equity* (Aguilar, 2020), we strongly suggest it. In her book, Elena Aguilar empowers leaders with strategies to

- Talk productively about race, power, and systems of oppression.
- Build trust to support vulnerability.
- Unpack mental models and change someone's mind.
- Observe classrooms and collect data to support equitable outcomes.
- Inspire others and deepen commitment.
- Evaluate and celebrate growth.

Creating an effective structure for coaching, feedback, and individualized professional development is a great way to combat the frustration experienced by teachers who deal with a lack of feedback from administrators (Gomez, n.d.). Don't just take it from us; check out this reflection from one of our teachers:

> Just like my first coaching session, I left my IPD day feeling refreshed and inspired. I have felt really drained since break—I got very used to my routine at home with my kids and it has been challenging to come back, so I appreciated this opportunity to recenter myself around

my work and philosophy. I really appreciate our coaching sessions because it is nice to get facetime with admin. I feel like my voice is definitely heard and my opinion is valued and taken into consideration. I appreciate how quickly I have been able to make a place for myself here and how welcome I feel! In our meeting, we talked about classroom management, in particular consequences and positive reinforcement. I came up with a plan that I can implement next week around positive reinforcement and a positive color chart (as we spoke). I'm hoping that this can be the solution and that the similarity to a negative color chart will be the beginning of students taking it seriously and that the positive reinforcement and rewards will help it to be successful.

When I met with Dr. Donnelly, I was able to focus on my spiritual health, which is an area where I have the least "character development"—that is to say, it is likely the area of my life I have spent the least amount of time intentionally cultivating. I feel so privileged to work for an organization that gives me time with a mental health professional that I can use at my own discretion with no stipulations; that time is very meaningful to me and it makes me respect and feel the magic of [our school] that much more.

I was able to observe the peers on my team to get a better sense of what they do for transitions and their general sense of "calm." I am reflecting the most on my own energy levels and how "protecting my energy" is a practice I will need to be intentional about but that will see meaningful results in both my professional and personal life. More controlled energy in the classroom means smoother and calmer classroom management, which means more energy at home with my family, which then invests in their social and emotional growth as well. Everyone wins when you take time for yourself and your mental health. I was also able to observe my wonderful mentor again and was so struck by how comfortable her students were with her and how natural she is with them. She is truly a magnificent person I look up to a lot. I would like to think the "stars" aligned for me to get this position after working with her but that would be discrediting my hard work and the relationships I built here.

I chose to use my digital learning time to take a deeper dive into positive reinforcement training and classroom management. The JCPS stream had a number of videos that gave me suggestions and reinforced ideas I already had. It is also comforting to take a page from the district in terms of discipline, and it feels good to know I am aligned with expectations, particularly as a new teacher.

One of the best ways you can mitigate teacher burnout is by making sure you have systems in place to nourish and support your current teachers so they don't end up feeling like Ms. Rodriguez (from the beginning of this chapter). One-on-one time with your teachers will help support them both professionally and personally. After all, if your goal is teaching the whole student, shouldn't it also be supporting the whole teacher?

Think-Abouts

1. What is your current culture of coaching? Does everyone get an opportunity for coaching?
2. How do you utilize your master schedule and support personnel to support your coaching structure?
3. How do you structure your beginning-of-the-year meetings to set the tone for teacher growth and development?
4. What does your system for peer observation look like?
5. What actions are you taking to ensure your entire coaching team has a common understanding of your coaching and feedback system? Is your feedback and walkthrough system sustainable? Does your coaching team have a common understanding of the system?
6. How are you supporting your teachers personally?
7. What data do you use to create your professional development plan? How do you ensure differentiated opportunities for your staff?

6

Work-Life Balance

"Love yourself enough to set boundaries. Your time and energy are precious. You get to choose how you use it. You teach people how to treat you by deciding what you will and won't accept."

—Anna Taylor

> 🔋 **Burnout Challenge**
>
> Teacher workdays have always been full of responsibilities, but teacher shortages and decreased planning time have increased an already heavy workload. The increased demands placed on teachers to do more with less leaves them feeling overwhelmed, overworked, and exhausted. The extra responsibilities also spill over into their home life, leaving less time to spend with family, which causes feelings of resentment and a loss of passion for what they do.

Ms. Martinez, an 11th grade language arts teacher, found herself trapped in an unyielding cycle of work. Long hours, endless lesson planning, and the constant demands of her profession left her feeling frustrated and drained. The lack of a work-life balance had taken its toll, and she yearned to reclaim a sense of harmony in her life.

One evening, as Ms. Martinez sat at her desk, buried under a pile of papers, she came to a realization that she could not continue to live like this. She was constantly trying to get caught up not just with work but also with her own kids and their after-school activities. Feeling more than overwhelmed, Ms. Martinez let her principal know that she would be taking the following day off. It was time to make a plan. She couldn't continue to exhaust all her energy, leaving nothing for herself at the end of each day.

Creating a healthy work-life balance is an area in which all school staff can probably use support. Even though there will always be those days or weeks in which work requires more in terms of the balance scale (think deadlines for budget, school improvement plans, evaluations, report cards, growth plans, family engagement event planning), we also know that if we allowed it, work would consume all our time—leaving us with an empty cup for our families, friends, and selves.

Although most educators understand the importance of a work-life balance, Babin Dhas and Karthikeyan (2015) outlined five measurable outcomes: personal and sick time saved, retention, motivation, absenteeism, and illnesses. As you consider these, first think about how each of these five outcomes affect your building. Are there teachers who use a significant amount of sick time due to illness or a lack of motivation? Is teacher retention an issue in your building? These questions are not to place blame, but we need to be honest with ourselves before we can make change. This chapter offers a variety of strategies to help support a healthy work-life balance you can implement as you see fit with your staff and school.

So how do we achieve a better work-life balance? Our experience is that you must be intentional about it or your scales will always tip toward the side of work. With that in mind, this chapter is organized by (1) important practices and (2) systems and structures. Important practices refer to the strategies that can support a healthy work-life balance on a personal level. These are things you can embed into your newsletter or add as a "tip of the week" to your faculty meetings. Although talking about these strategies is important, your actions speak louder than words. Therefore, if you model the strategies, it will make staff more inclined to give them a try. These strategies are also important for you to practice as an administrator because leadership burnout is just as prevalent as teacher burnout (Luhombo et al., 2023). In 2017 alone, 18 percent of public school principals resigned from their positions.

The second half of this chapter is dedicated to ways you can support your staff through the systems and structures in your building and district. You may not have direct control over all these practices, but they still provide a good place to start and serve as a guide to support your teachers in a systematic way.

Important Practices
Schedule Personal Time

So many times, when we talk with people about taking time for themselves, they say they don't have the time. Time is limited after work for so many of us because of family responsibilities, caring for loved ones, continued learning, and so much more. Scheduling time just for yourself is a great way to prioritize your well-being. Make it a priority. Schedule it in your calendar as an appointment with yourself to avoid conflicts with work-related business—or canceling on yourself.

Learn to Say *No*

Evaluate your priorities at work and home, and try to shorten your to-do list. Cut or delegate activities you don't enjoy or can't handle—or share your concerns and possible solutions with others, including your employer. When you stop accepting tasks out of guilt or from a false sense of obligation, you'll have more time for activities that are meaningful to you.

Choose a "Quitting Time" and Stick to It

How many teachers and administrators do you know who stay after work for a few hours or come in an hour early every day? How many send you emails at 9:00 p.m.—or later? There will always be more work to do in education. The work is never finished. The truth is you could work 14 hours a day and still not feel caught up. Instead of burning yourself out by constantly working, choose an end time for the day and stick to it. Here's the important part, though: Once that time comes, pack up your things and go home. Don't find excuses to delay. And once you get home, *be home.*

Turn On "Do Not Disturb"

Most smartphones have a "do not disturb" feature that is particularly helpful when you are spending time with family or loved ones and, well, don't want to be disturbed. It's also helpful when you need to prioritize sleep. It's far too easy to stay up late working. Don't fall into that trap. Turning on "do not disturb" helps you get uninterrupted time to spend with your family or get a good night's sleep.

We get it. This is a drastic step for many people. You may be a little fearful of turning on "do not disturb," especially if you have kids who live away from home or a dependent family member. Fear not. You can override this feature for emergencies and specific people you want to always get through to you. Most phones allow you to select contacts whose phone calls and texts will still ring or send notifications—even with "do not disturb" turned on. This is a great feature that can give you peace of mind while still setting boundaries with your time.

Put Your Phone Down at Dinner or with Family

Earlier, we said, "Once you are home, *be home.*" This is exactly what we mean when we say that. After a difficult day, there may still be follow-up conversations required to prepare for the next day. However, your family also deserves your time, attention, and presence. Prioritize your time with them by putting your phone down during dinner and family time. The follow-up work conversations can wait.

Uninstall Your Work Email from Your Phone

Take a deep breath. If you're like us, you probably just had major anxiety reading that heading. Deleting your work email account sounds really scary because so many of us rely on email to be accessible at all times. However, think about it. If you're really needed by a coworker or superior, will they email you? No. They'll call or send a text. Let's be clear: You will not miss an emergency sent through email.

Deleting or uninstalling your work email account from your phone sets a clear boundary with how frequently you can check it. How many times have you been in the middle of a conversation with someone but instead of listening, you were reading your email? This can be true all day long if your email is easily accessible on your phone. Deleting it not only sets clear boundaries but also allows you to be more present in each moment of the day—whether that is in conversations with coworkers, teaching content, making observations, planning, and so much more.

Make a List of What Constitutes an Emergency

What could potentially happen at night that would pull you away from your family? What absolutely couldn't wait until the morning? What needs your attention immediately? Think of those scenarios, and then make it a priority to stick to that list only. Everything else can wait until the following day. Most of the time, no one *really* needs you at 11 p.m. There aren't many true after-hours emergencies for educators. Really think about this and create a list for yourself. Write it down as a constant reminder when you are considering responding to something after your work hours. Use the list to hold yourself accountable. In addition, make sure you communicate these hypothetical scenarios with your staff. If your staff are used to getting an immediate response from you at all hours of the night, let them know that you are not suddenly ignoring them. Rather, you are setting boundaries to prioritize your own family while at home. Modeling this behavior gives them permission to do the same.

Recognize the Difference Between Progress and Perfection

By and large, educators are passionate about their jobs and recognize the importance of educating students to be prepared for life. However, sometimes the will to do a great job turns into perfectionism. Perfectionism can motivate staff to try their best, but it can also create a spiral in which nothing is ever good enough. The need to be perfect also eliminates the creative freedom to try something new because of a fear of failure. Think about your staff for a minute. Is there a culture of perfectionism in your school? Do you have teachers who are willing to try something new? What do your teachers assume of your expectations? Many times, the high expectations we set for ourselves and our staff can be perceived as a need for perfection.

Creating and supporting a culture of "failing forward" can be incredibly difficult when so much is on the line for schools in terms of test scores. However, as the world around us changes through innovation, educators must be willing to try new ways of doing things. To support this culture as an administrator, be sure to call out yourself when you make a mistake. Instead of falling prey to the negative self-talk that typically goes along with failure, acknowledge how the mistake can support your growth as a person and professional. Again, when administrators model this behavior, it makes it less risky for teachers to do the same.

Mean What You Say

Did you grow up hearing the saying "Do as I say, not as I do"? Many of us are great about saying the right thing and coaching others to make good choices for themselves. However, we find it much more difficult to do the same for ourselves. It is important to ensure that, as a leader, you don't send mixed signals about your expectations. Your words and actions should be aligned to demonstrate active support for your teachers in the most holistic way possible.

Have you ever worked with a leader who said things such as "Have a restful break, but can you also do these five things for me before you return?" Have you done this yourself? It's OK. We've all been guilty of this at some point. Moving forward, though, you should make it a priority not to expect people to work over a break—especially after you said to get some rest.

So? How is your current work-life balance? Does your schedule promote or hinder a healthy balance? What about your teachers? Do they have a work-life balance? Reflect on your current practices, and challenge yourself to make a plan to move forward.

Systems and Structures
Give the Gift of Time

Imagine you are in a room with 100 other educators. Someone asks if you need more time during the day. How many people do you think would raise their hands? Almost everyone, right? The gift of time, especially in education, is beyond precious. Unfortunately, time is one resource we cannot create or get more of. However, the gift of time is about supporting teachers' use of time they do have in the most efficient way possible.

In Chapter 2, we discussed systems and structures for collaboration and how they support the overall well-being of staff. For example, collaborative planning and unit planning days significantly reduce the amount of outside time teachers need for planning purposes. Even though these systems don't completely eliminate the need for planning, they help the work get divided among team members so they can work more efficiently.

There are other ways to give the gift of time. One of the most important is to limit meetings as much as possible, especially meetings that take place after hours or that are not crucial to the school's vision or mission. If you can send an email instead of gathering everyone together, do that. If you are worried that your email will go unread, explain to staff that you are trying to value their time. Share with them that, instead of making them come to a meeting, you would much rather send an email whenever possible. Setting this purpose will not only give your staff a greater appreciation for the intent but also encourage them to follow through and read the email.

One of the most important questions an administrator can ask or analyze is this: What can I take off your plate?

More than ever, teachers are being asked to do more with the same amount of time. Are there specific tasks your teachers are doing that could or should be done by someone else? For example, in our building, teachers were creating agendas for their PLC time. That may seem like a small task, but it was something the instructional coach could create and then distribute to teachers for review or edits before the meeting. There are so many small things like this that can be taken off teachers' plates. Taken together, all those small things free up a significant amount of time.

Implement an Employee Assistance Program

Employee assistance programs (EAP) are mental health supports typically funded by the school district. If you have access to an EAP, make sure the relevant information is included in at least one weekly newsletter or posted in a common area of the school. Refer to it often. This resource is hugely important for employees who may be struggling mentally or emotionally. The purpose of an EAP is to quickly connect employees with someone so they do not have to spend their time and energy trying to locate a therapist or mental health professional who accepts their insurance and has availability. Another benefit of an EAP is that visits can often be held virtually or by phone, thereby saving the employee even more time (that would be spent traveling to and from appointments). They can more or less immediately get the help they need.

If your district does not have an EAP, here are a few resources available throughout the United States:

- National Hotline for Suicide Prevention (dial 988): This is for people in dire need of immediate mental and emotional support.
- *Psychology Today* (www.psychologytoday.com): This is useful to locate therapists in your area. You can filter by insurance, age, availability, and more.
- Better Help (www.betterhelp.com): This service helps you find a virtual therapist so you can access therapy from wherever you are located.

As the world changes, so does the field of education. Nevertheless, there is one thing that will likely remain the same: the need for a healthy work-life balance. Although we know that the scales will not always be evenly balanced, taking time to rest is incredibly important for both your staff and yourself. Focusing on important practices and the systems and structures your school has in place is imperative to creating a culture in which work-life balance is not only discussed but also actively practiced and supported. This helps support the mental and emotional health of educators in your building, and it helps reduce absenteeism and retain high-quality teachers. In addition, it significantly reduces the stress felt by administrators like you.

Think-Abouts

1. What teachers or teams struggle the most with absenteeism? Is this due to illness? How might you support that teacher or team specifically?

2. How do you currently model a healthy work-life balance?

3. Does your district fund an employee assistance program? If so, how could you add a reminder of this program so staff are aware of this resource? If not, what other resources could you provide or suggest?

PART III

Immediate Action to
Triage Emotional
Labor and Exhaustion

7

Appreciation

"A person who feels appreciated will always do more than what is expected."

—Anonymous

> 🔋 **Burnout Challenge**
>
> In addition to feeling overworked and overwhelmed, teachers feel unappreciated for all the extra roles and responsibilities they have to assume.

The staff at Bensenville Middle School had always been dedicated to collaboration to do whatever it takes for their students, families, and one another. Their former principal created an atmosphere that made "going the extra mile" part of the school's culture. In addition to teaching their own classes, many staff members coached or sponsored before- and after-school clubs and extracurriculars, volunteered for committees, and attended many of the family engagement events. Since Mrs. Hampshire became the principal, however, there had been a steady decline in extra involvement.

Concerned by this decline, one of the assistant principals, Ms. Huff, who had been at Bensenville for more than 10 years, met with some of the teachers to investigate. Through their discussions, she discovered that the

teachers felt as though the new principal failed to take time to build relationships with them while also requiring more meetings and paperwork,
much of which felt compliance driven.

One teacher said, "We love our students and families here at Bensenville and are willing to do whatever it takes; however, it seems like we are
just being directed to do all of these extra things without any understanding of why, which has left us feeling undervalued and unappreciated."

This is most likely a familiar sentiment. In addition to feeling overworked and overwhelmed, many teachers also feel unappreciated (Molero
et al., 2019), making all the extra roles and responsibilities they have to
assume less than desirable. If you were to do a quick poll among your staff,
how would they say they feel?

Think about the last time you did something for someone else and
they demonstrated their appreciation through words or gifts. Now think
about the last time you did something for someone else and it wasn't even
acknowledged. It often leaves lingering questions. Did they not like what
you did or how you did it? Leaving staff with similar questions adds unnecessary stress to an already overflowing plate. By acknowledging the work
that our staff is doing well, we can help remove that specific stress and take
one more thing off their plate.

We understand how powerful it can be to feel appreciated and make
others feel appreciated. The power of gratitude and affirmation is incalcu-
lable. We've sent emails, given cards, shared small tokens of appreciation,
and stopped by teachers' classrooms to tell them know how grateful we
are for things such as coaching the volleyball team, creating a schoolwide
spreadsheet, or taking time after school to make a home visit. These things
remain important, but in 2016, the culture of our district required that we
step our appreciation game up to the next level.

During that tumultuous time, top-down district micromanaging had
never been higher. On top of the normal pressures of being an educator—including district and state mandates, high-stakes accountability, and
typical student and family stressors—our district made the decision to hire

an outside agency to conduct a salary study. You read right. In a time when everyone was already feeling overworked and underpaid, we received the message that "You might be making too much money, so we might decide to cut your salary." As you can imagine, this felt like the ultimate slap in the face. As leaders, there are things we can control—and things we cannot. Although the salary study was beyond our control, we knew we had to act fast if we wanted to mitigate the toxic impact a potential salary decrease would have on our staff.

In this chapter, we share some of the strategies we used (and continue to use) to ensure our staff members feel appreciated, which has resulted in a very high retention rate. We know that many of these ideas support appreciation, but none of these ideas alone will change your entire school climate and culture. However, they will support teacher retention and take your culture to the next level when combined with the systems and structures in Parts I and II.

Teacher attrition is only growing as a universal problem in education, so one of the ways you can help retain high-quality teachers is by making them feel appreciated. An astonishing 64 percent of Americans who leave their job say they do so because they don't feel appreciated (Chapman & White, 2019). Therefore, the ideas outlined in this chapter are meant to be a helpful (nonexhaustive) guide you can reference at any time as you make an intentional plan to support teacher appreciation.

Appreciate Your Staff
Staff Spotlight

Often, when staff awards are given out, they go to the same people every time. Yes, the rock stars in your school always deserve recognition, but the purpose of a staff spotlight is to vary the acknowledgment. Every week, during our administrative team meetings, we have a standing agenda item to discuss which staff member has gone above and beyond that week. Here are some of the things we consider when selecting this person to acknowledge:

- Who was faced with—and overcame—an extra-tough challenge with a parent?
- Who has shown up to work every day, despite dealing with something really heavy outside school?
- Who has gone above and beyond by demonstrating one of our school's core values?
- Who was responsible for picking up the slack of an absent teammate?

Regardless of the criteria you use, staff spotlights are a great way to make people feel appreciated. Another possibility is to have a weekly submission (either with a paper form or digitally through something like a Google Form) for staff to nominate one of their peers. The truth is that, as administrators, we don't always know everything that is happening within team meetings, with classroom instruction, or with collaboration. Teachers and staff are more familiar with the "behind-the-scenes" efforts since they work closely with one another every day. Asking staff to submit their colleagues for recognition, then, boosts morale and encourages staff to celebrate one another—and themselves.

Once a recipient is selected, they can be celebrated in a variety of ways. For example, our instructional coach highlights the spotlight recipient in her weekly newsletter with a photo and rationale for the recognition (see Figure 7.1). It's also printed out and hung outside the staff member's room so that anyone who comes in the building can see the recognition. Next, we post it on the social media platform we use for professional communication. This lets other educators or anyone who follows our school know who is being recognized and why. Finally, we post the recognition on Facebook, which is what most of our employees use for more of a personal form of social media. This extends the appreciation and highlights them not only in their professional community but also in their personal community. Posting on multiple platforms heightens the awareness of the recognition and allows colleagues, friends, and family to make supportive—and public—comments, further enhancing the impact of appreciation.

FIGURE 7.1
Example Staff Spotlight

Kenwood Staff Spotlight: Lara Donnelly

Position: Counselor

Education: Bachelor's in Elementary Education & Special Education, Master's and Educational Specialist in Professional School Counseling, Doctorate in Educational Leadership

Hobbies/Interests: Playing with my daughter, cycling, running

Favorite Book: *The Magic*

Favorite Quote: Wake up each day with a grateful heart.

Extra Info: I love to learn and grow!

Lara works hard to build staff culture and climate in addition to her counseling role for students and families. Lara leads our family engagement efforts and has started an initiative with our first-ever Parent Ambassador group.

Staff Shout-Outs

Many people are familiar with social media shout-outs, but this appreciation idea has a unique spin to it. At the beginning of the year, we create a Google Form and share the link with everyone (staff, students, families, and community stakeholders). They can then submit a shout-out for someone on staff who they feel has gone above and beyond. In an effort to ensure that all stakeholders have access to submit a shout-out, we create a QR code, display it in common areas of the building, and routinely add it to newsletters. The goal here is to make it as easy as possible for people to give a staff member praise and kudos.

Often, staff will send a shout-out to a peer as thanks for helping with a specific task. Other times, it is more personal message (e.g., "Thank you for taking my students at the end of the day when my own child was sick"). At the end of every week, all shout-outs are added to an administrator's newsletter or slide deck so the entire staff can see all the messages. This helps provide a collective celebration among staff.

The unfortunate truth is that, occasionally, staff members and their contributions can get overlooked. If you notice that there is a particular person who often gets overlooked and doesn't receive a staff shout-out, see if there are ways to help provide a sense of belonging for that person. This may not be the case in every building, but you may need to pay attention and provide more support so *all* staff feel connected with the school community.

Appreciation Carts

Few things spark joy like an unexpected treat after a rough day or week. Appreciation carts provide an opportunity for administrators to be visible and display their gratitude. The idea behind an appreciation cart is to offer a variety of feel-good trinkets, verbally show gratitude to staff, or share a printed note of encouragement. The cart could contain items for a coffee bar. It could have chips and chocolate. It could have doughnuts. It could have popcorn and cold soda. (You might be surprised at how much gratitude an unexpected cold soda can bring.) It could be a variety of things. The point is that it's a small, surprising, and welcome show of appreciation.

Consider creating a theme around an upcoming holiday or tailoring it specifically to your staff by using a quote or play on words. For example, if your message is "We appreciate you to pieces," there are countless candy, snack, and decorative options that go along with that phrase. Regardless of what you choose to include on your appreciation cart, the point is that you are letting people know, "Hey, we see you and we appreciate you."

Although we vary the types of trinkets or snacks we put on our carts, we *always* include quotes. While preparing the carts, we find a variety of quotes that really speak to us. We print out small copies of the quotes and put them in a basket for teachers to take when they choose their goodies. Sometimes teachers choose them intentionally by looking through the basket and saying, "This is the one that spoke to me." Other times, we mix them up and teachers choose them randomly. Occasionally, we place a star or other symbol on the back of a quote for an additional prize (usually a gift card to a local coffee shop or restaurant). Although we'd love to give out gift cards to everyone, that can get costly. A random drawing with the possibility of an "extra" prize typically generates even more excitement as we take the appreciation cart around the school.

Appreciation carts are just a little extra something to remind our staff how much we care about and support them. They can be scheduled ahead of time (e.g., the last Friday of the month), but more often than not, we spontaneously take the carts out when we feel things getting heavy. Sometimes that heaviness is rooted in recurring events (e.g., right after report cards or schoolwide testing); other times, it is caused by district mandates or larger community/societal issues that affect staff and students. Regardless, the purpose of appreciation carts is to make sure we mitigate the heavy lifting our staff must endure. Trust us—the responses you get when your teachers open the door to see the appreciation cart is priceless.

Room Service

This gesture of appreciation is similar to appreciation carts but provides a more personal touch. When teachers arrive to school in the morning, they find a door hanger on their classroom door with a menu of options for drinks and snacks—and a preferred time of delivery. They fill out their order and send it to the office with their attendance folder. Although a handwritten order form has a more personal touch, this could be done through an online form if you are running really low on time. The admin team then fulfills the orders and delivers them at the requested times by knocking on the door and saying, "Room service!"

To lay the groundwork for this, we ask staff complete a survey at the beginning of the school year that indicates their favorite snacks, drinks, restaurants, places to shop, and so on (Figure 7.2). We then use this information throughout the year as we choose items for our appreciation carts and room service.

FIGURE 7.2
Staff Favorites Survey

Staff Favorites	Response
Name	
What is your monogram (initial order: first, middle, last)?	
What is your favorite drink?	
What is your favorite snack?	
What are your hobbies?	
Where is your favorite place to shop?	
Where is your favorite place to eat lunch?	
What is your favorite color?	
What is your favorite candy/sweet treat?	
Is there anything else you would like to share?	

When we distribute appreciation carts and room service, we often hear students ask, "Hey, how come she's getting something and we're not?" We always respond, "This treat is to make sure your teacher knows she is appreciated." Then we ask the students, "What do you think you can do to make your teacher feel a little more appreciated?" Planting that seed helps reap an extra level of appreciation from those who matter most—our students.

Individualized and Group Appreciation

As mentioned, the staff favorites survey responses drive many of our appreciation efforts. We don't keep all that information to ourselves, though. Typically, we transfer all the responses to a shared spreadsheet so it is easily readable and accessible. This is distributed to the entire staff so anyone can surprise a coworker with one of their favorite drinks or snacks. This is immensely helpful when we want to individualize our appreciation. For example, if a staff member has gone above and beyond and we want to recognize those efforts, we may handwrite a note and purchase something from their favorites list to surprise them. Showing appreciation in this way is much more intentional than giving a generic gift card or trinket they may not care about or be able to use.

Throughout the school year, teachers set individual goals for student growth on common formative assessments, district assessments, and more. Individualized recognition is a great way to show appreciation for the intentionality in their work. However, sometimes an entire team may excel at helping students grow, supporting families, or engaging community stakeholders. When a team goes above and beyond, group appreciation can help reinforce and encourage the collective efforts of each member. What does this look like? It could be giving them public recognition on the morning announcements, handwriting a note to the team calling out how team members contributed to reach their goal, providing favorite snacks at their next team meeting, or giving gift cards they can use for a team outing.

The opportunities for individual and group appreciation are endless. The most important aspect of this type of appreciation is making sure it is intentional rather than generic. Intentional appreciation helps build—and can help improve—a great school culture.

Guest Teacher Appreciation

Most schools are facing teacher and substitute shortages. We absolutely understand the challenge of finding coverage when multiple teachers are out on a particular day. In Chapter 10, we discuss the system we put in place to address this with our current staff. We use a rotating roster of non-homeroom teachers who can be tapped to be a guest teacher (what we call substitutes in our building) for the day. We therefore set up an additional system of appreciation for this specific purpose.

Non-homeroom teachers have very specific and important roles in supporting students. When they are required to be a guest teacher for the day, it disrupts their day and the students with whom they work. When they are asked to be a guest teacher, they receive a grab bag of snacks and a raffle ticket that enters them into a weekly or monthly drawing for a gift card to a local restaurant or coffee shop. The grab bag and raffle ticket do not disrupt their day any less, but it gives them an immediate token of gratitude—because the school literally could not function smoothly without them that day!

Make an Appreciation Plan

Sporadic appreciation can go a long way, but the truth is that school leaders rarely have days that aren't jam packed. Therefore, if you do not have a plan for appreciation, it may not happen. You may think that planning for appreciation takes away its spontaneity and genuine nature, but it most certainly does not! If you have at least one form of appreciation tentatively planned for each month, you still have the freedom to be as flexible as needed and respond to specific needs as they arise. For example, the beginning-of-the-year enthusiasm typically starts to wane a little by October. Students and staff are both settled in, and student behavior issues typically start to increase. That makes October an important month for appreciation, so it's a good idea to plan specific appreciation strategies you want to use in October—knowing that the extra appreciation will go a long way. See Figure 7.3 for an example of an appreciation plan.

What goes into an appreciation plan? Teamann and Miller (2019) suggest planning at least one idea per month with the following information already outlined:

- Appreciation idea
- Person responsible
- Funding source

FIGURE 7.3

Sample Appreciation Plan

Month	Appreciation Idea/Day	Preparation Needed	Person Responsible	Funding Source
	Room Service	• Purchase snacks • Print room service templates	Principal	PTA collaboration
	Staff Spotlight of the Week	• Google Form • Add to social media	Assistant principal	N/A
	Staff Shout-Outs	• Google Form • Add to weekly newsletter	Instructional coach	N/A
October	Cancel a Faculty Meeting	• Communicate to staff that they will have one less meeting to appreciate their time	Principal	N/A
	National Principal Month	• Create flyer to celebrate	Counselor	PTA collaboration
	School Custodian Appreciation Day	• Create flyer to celebrate	Assistant principal	Donations from community partners
	National Coach Day	• Create flyer to celebrate	Principal	Donations from community partners

Designating the person responsible allows everyone on the administration team to be involved and ensures that one person is not always taking on the lion's share of work. The funding source is even more critical. Some leaders have 150 employees. One appreciation cart or room service day could get expensive very quickly. Some possible funding sources could include your PTA/PTO or collaborative community partners (willing to donate items such as coffee, gift cards, and light snacks). In an effort to sustain a reciprocal relationship with willing community partners, we try to support their local business as much as possible when planning school events so we are not always just asking for things.

For your convenience, the following is a list of national appreciation days or weeks that are related to school staff. If you search for these days online, you'll find great graphics and the exact dates for the current year:

- National IT Professional Day
- National Principal Month
- School Custodian Appreciation Day
- National Coach Day
- National School Psychologist Week
- National Education Support Professionals Day
- School Bus Driver Appreciation Week/School Bus Safety Awareness
- National Substitute Appreciation Day
- School Resource Officer Appreciation Day
- National School Counseling Week
- Maintenance Worker Appreciation Day
- National School Social Worker Week
- School Librarian Appreciation Day
- National Assistant Principal Week
- Paraprofessional Appreciation Day
- School Bus Driver Appreciation Day
- National Administrative Professionals Day
- School Principal's Day
- Teacher Appreciation Week

- School Lunch Hero Day
- School Nurse Day
- Speech Pathologist Day

Understanding Appreciation

We feel it's important to mention that words of appreciation and acknowledgment still go a long way. When we walk into our teachers' classrooms, we see notes we left for them years ago. This is not surprising considering almost half of the people surveyed by Chapman and White (2019) identify words of appreciation as their preferred method of appreciation in the workplace.

Some people feel uncomfortable if they are recognized or appreciated in front of a large group. For people who prefer to be recognized in a more intimate setting, stopping by their room in the morning, before the day starts, or acknowledging them during a one-on-one coaching session is a great way to meet their needs. Others prefer to be thanked in front of a small group. You can offer an appropriate level of appreciation to those individuals during a PLC, for example. For some staff members, the bigger the audience, the better. For them, a staff meeting might be a great time to offer verbal recognition and appreciation.

By contrast, some people prefer any appreciation they receive to be written. Knowing your staff—and whether they prefer public or private acknowledgment or spoken or written appreciation—can add an invaluable personal touch. Any level of appreciation is better than no appreciation, but understanding and recognizing people's preferred appreciation language can help you make the gestures more meaningful.

Does this mean we must always individualize and vary every act of appreciation? No. Does this mean we must be more intentional when we deliver words of appreciation? Absolutely. At the end of the day, being intentional with your actions—to let your staff know you appreciate the big and small things they do—is critical. Gratitude goes a long way, and it can be contagious.

In addition to words of appreciation, Chapman and White (2019) also identify quality time as one of the highest forms of appreciation in the workplace. This isn't something administrators typically have in abundance, yet there are ways to think of and address the gift of quality time. As mentioned, it's important to protect teacher time as much as possible. For example, if a meeting isn't absolutely necessary, cancel it. Don't waste time simply because a meeting was scheduled. If it's not necessary, it's not necessary! Shifting this perspective and protecting teacher time is an incredible way to show appreciation.

A question we often hear is some variation of "How do you find the time to do all this?" Honestly, the time it takes to implement and carry out some of these ideas varies. See Figure 7.4 to get a better idea of what you will need and the estimated amount of time (for 80–100 staff members). Administrators aren't sitting around looking for more things to do. However, the saying "You make time for what is important" could not be more relevant. If you believe in showing gratitude and appreciation to your staff for the work they do every day with students, then you will make the time.

Although Ms. Huff was concerned about how the new principal, Mrs. Hampshire, would react to the information she gained through her meetings with teachers, she knew it was a crucial conversation that needed to happen. Ms. Huff shared the concerns with Mrs. Hampshire and asked how she could help turn things around.

"I had no idea everyone felt like this," said Mrs. Hampshire. "I've been under a lot of pressure from the district to make sure our test scores don't drop, so I instituted some of the successful strategies I used at my previous school to support our continuous improvement. I guess I moved too fast without considering the needs of the teachers. They work so hard; I don't want them to feel unappreciated. What can I do?"

In response, Mrs. Hampshire, Ms. Huff, and the rest of the administrative staff met to create a staff appreciation plan for the rest of the year and committed to revisiting it during the summer to update it as a yearlong plan. This would ensure they embedded staff appreciation as part of their school culture.

FIGURE 7.4 **Appreciation Ideas**		
Appreciation Idea	**What You Need**	**Estimated Time**
Staff Spotlight	• Digital template • Method for sharing • *Optional:* Google Form for staff submissions	20 minutes total
Staff Shout-Outs	• Google Form for capturing shout-outs • QR code to make the form easily accessible • Weekly administration newsletter to include the shout-outs	10 minutes weekly
Appreciation Cart	• Snacks, drinks, or trinkets • Printed quotes • Cart for delivery • *Optional:* Two or three $5 to $10 gift cards to local restaurants/coffee shops	2 to 3 hours (depending on the size of your staff and building)
Room Service	• Printed room service door hanger or form • Snacks, drinks, or trinkets • Delivery system	2 to 3 hours (depending on the size of your staff and building)
Guest Teacher Appreciation	• Snacks • Grab bags • Raffle tickets • Container to collect the raffle tickets	30 minutes for prep time 1 to 2 minutes to distribute

Think-Abouts

1. How do you currently make your staff feel appreciated?
2. How could you determine the preferred appreciation language of each of your staff members?
3. What could you include in a yearlong plan for appreciation that is sustainable for you and your administration team?
4. How can you collaborate with community partners to support your appreciation ideas?

8

Fun in the Workplace

*"Fun is at the core of the way I like to do business, and it has been
key to everything I've done from the outset. More than any
other element, fun is the secret of Virgin's success."*

—Richard Branson

> **Burnout Challenge**
>
> The daily workload of teaching is heightened by the plethora of negative narratives about education that appear on social media. These anecdotes create mental and emotional fatigue and can lead to a culture of negativity.

Mrs. Anderson, a passionate teacher, noticed her fellow teachers were exhausted and morale was at its lowest. She could feel it in herself, too. It was more than the typical feeling of being drained in the middle of the school year. Trying to think of possible solutions, she thought about all the end-of-year fun activities that make those days fly by! With that in mind, she started imagining what a day like that could look like in the middle of the school year.

The next day, Mrs. Anderson dropped by her principal's office to propose the idea of a "fun day" to inject joy into their work lives. As they discussed it, the principal shared all the reasons why it would be difficult: there is so much to do before testing, staff may not be interested, and—most important—who would cover the costs? Knowing that something big had to change, Mrs. Anderson asked one more time just to give it a chance. The principal said she would support the idea but only if Mrs. Anderson planned the activities and took care of the logistics.

With the principal's approval, Mrs. Anderson got to work by determining staff preferences. Knowing she couldn't take on the full magnitude of the work because she also didn't have time for "one more thing," she reached out to the school's PTA and a few community organizations to see if they could help. Excited for the opportunity to support the school, a committee of community partners formed and delegated roles and responsibilities to make sure the staff got exactly what they needed to rejuvenate and prepare for the rest of the school year.

Fun Day arrived, transforming the staff room and injecting some much-needed vibrancy into the school culture. Icebreakers, art, outdoor games, and a talent show filled the day with laughter. Exhaustion melted away and was replaced by a renewed sense of energy and camaraderie. The impact lingered, fostering a vibrant and motivated teaching team that helped carry them through the second half of the year. Students benefited, too, as teachers' renewed energies found their way into their classrooms.

In the previous chapter, we discussed the importance of appreciation in the workplace. This chapter focuses on a component that is equally important and can help remove stress from your employees' plate: having fun at work. When someone suggests trying to "have fun" with your staff, you may automatically think "icebreaker." Let's be real, though. How many times have you taken part in an icebreaker activity, whether it was in a college course, during professional development, or in staff meetings? You've probably lost count. Each time the word is mentioned, there is always an audible groan in objection.

We're not using the term *icebreaker* here because this chapter isn't about basic introductions between colleagues or coworkers. Rather, we want to help you intentionally build and foster positive working relationships. With the countless demands educators have on their collective plates, it's easy to take ourselves too seriously. Sometimes, though, we just need to be reminded of the joys of play.

Studies have revealed that employees who have fun in the workplace take less sick leave, work harder, and are more productive (BrightHR, 2016). In addition, if fun in the workplace is presented in an organic way with considerations for culture and identity, it can increase motivation and productivity while decreasing stress (Everett, 2011).

As leaders, we are faced with daily challenges we must overcome, and one of the challenges that most often plagues our district (and probably yours) is a lack of teachers and substitutes. We know there are obstacles that are more challenging than a lack of substitutes, but when you have three to five classrooms without substitutes for the day, that's a challenge—and it's not a fun one to have.

If there's a way to lessen teacher absences and help people take less sick leave, sign us up! This chapter, therefore, offers a range of ways to promote fun with your staff in meaningful ways, regardless of your budget and within the scope of possibility for any school administrator.

Intentional Fun

Having fun for the sake of having fun can be a great time. However, if you are like most administrators, you probably have a shortage of time and see this as not terribly productive. By contrast, having fun for an intentional purpose can provide a lot of value for the allotted time you give it. As we explore different activities to promote fun in this chapter, you'll notice there's a range in activity length. Some may only take one minute, whereas others, such as the ghost run, might need half a day. You read that right. Half a day. Don't worry, we'll explain why and how. Here are some of the ways in which we intentionally infuse fun into our school day.

First impressions set the tone for any relationship. Working relation- ships are no different. You have only one chance to make a first impression each school year. You may have new staff members, but even if you don't, all staff have spent the summer away from one another and spend the first few days of the school year catching up and reconnecting with coworkers. Prioritizing fun and team building on the first day back to school can help set the tone for the year. Think about a time when you were away from work for an extended period. Maybe it was due to illness. Maybe it was for maternity or paternity leave. Regardless of the reason, your return to work is hugely important. Being greeted with notes or a gift from colleagues say- ing they missed you strikes a different chord than coming back to a place where no one even acknowledged that you were gone.

Regardless of what district initiatives come down the pike or what required training you have been asked to give, don't just fall back into the routines of work. Set the tone for your staff by allowing them to have fun, strengthen bonds, and build trust with one another. The first day back is the most crucial time for this. Another important time for embedding fun is when you fall into a lull during the school year. It happens to everyone. It could be during a long stretch between breaks (e.g., the time between winter and spring breaks) or after a spate of negative press about teachers, education, or turmoil in your district. Whatever the reason, you'll know it is time to break up the routine and add fun when you feel complacency in your building.

The final justification for creating fun with staff might be the most important. As an administrator, you know there are times when it is cru- cial to have a faculty meeting. However, after working a full day, it can be difficult to take in or process new information. Therefore, incorporat- ing a short, fun activity before the meeting can help release endorphins and increase staff's willingness to listen, pay attention, and take in new information.

As you read, think about how each of the ideas in this chapter could be implemented or changed to meet the needs of your staff—and when they would be most valuable.

Ghost Run

If you aren't familiar with ghost runs, they're typically held around Halloween and are tons of fun. In the typical version, they're a bit like scavenger hunts. You show up to a beginning location and receive clues that take you throughout your city before eventually ending at a haunted house.

The school version of a ghost run can serve a variety of purposes. Not only can it promote fun, but it can (and really should, if possible) get your staff out into the community. Create clues that hint at community locations but do not name them outright. This can be done via typed, handwritten, or digital clues, depending on the complexity of your ghost run.

On the day of the event, all teams begin at the school and are given a starting clue. Decide if you want all teams to travel to the same locations in the same order or if you want to mix it up. Once they get to a location, determine a way for teams to verify that they are in the correct place (e.g., take a selfie, get a form signed off, collect a token or souvenir). If you want to involve community partners, you could have staff visit businesses to collect clues or ask community partners to hand out clues at various locations. If you are not quite there in terms of community partnerships, that's OK! This activity could help you build new relationships, but it does not have to rely on them.

Once all teams complete the ghost run and regroup at school, debrief and recap the experience to extend the fun. A recap in the form of slideshow or video can add to the fun, especially if some teams went to a wrong location or did something particularly silly. Allowing teams to debrief with one another helps them not only process the experience but also reflect on how much they learned about their community.

Human Hungry Hippos

The months of February and March have fewer breaks in the form of holidays. With state testing on the horizon, this time of year often presents challenges in maintaining a positive staff culture and climate. This activity is one that takes a bit of setup to put together, but it's a great activity to use when the energy is really heavy in the building. Even though it may take some more time to set up, it's more than worth it!

If you've played the classic children's board game Hungry Hungry Hippos, then you're already familiar with this concept. In the game, four hippos chomp into the middle of the board to snatch and eat marbles. For Human Hungry Hippos, you can have any number of players, along with the following materials:

- Rolling carts
- Milk crates or small boxes
- Inflated balloons
- *Optional:* Helmets to provide additional safety

To play, one staff member lies on their stomach on the rolling cart while holding a milk crate. Another staff member pushes the cart—and their partner—forward and backward to scoop up balloons in their milk crate. Whichever team catches the most balloons is the winner (which is also optional, depending on the competitive nature of your staff).

Giving staff the option to participate in a way that feels most comfortable is important in this game. Not everyone will want to lie on the cart or push someone else around. There are several options for staff who do not want to actively play the game. They could help keep the balloons in the middle of the room, count balloons as they are caught, or be a referee to make sure no team is sabotaging another. One of the unanticipated outcomes of this game is that it is almost impossible for staff to be in the same space as the game and *not* have a good time. Even if they are not actively participating at a given moment, just watching this game is so much fun.

Minute to Win It

Most people have seen, heard, or played some version of a "Minute to Win It" game. They're great to promote fun when you're short on time. Typically, we use these games when we can tell our staff seem tired or over-whelmed and we have something important to discuss in a staff meeting or training. Participating in a quick, fun game encourages laughter, releases endorphins, and can help staff be ready to receive information, especially after a long day of teaching. There are tons of these types of games, but the following are our (and our staff's) favorites.

Cookie Monster: The only item you need for this game is box of cookies. Have each person place a cookie on their forehead. Without using their hands, they must try and slide the cookie down their face and into their mouth. Set a timer for one minute. The first person to get their cookie in their mouth is the winner. And let's be honest: anyone who gets to enjoy a cookie is also a winner. The only modification we sometimes make is a consideration of dietary needs. If you have staff who are vegan or sugar free, find a box of appropriate cookies so everyone gets to enjoy a treat.

Stick with It: This game requires shaving cream, goggles, and cheese puffs. Have one staff member from each team wear the goggles and put shaving cream on their face. This may need to be you at first. Staff will be more willing to participate after watching you model. Have the rest of the team stand a designated distance away and toss cheese puffs, trying to get them to stick to the shaving cream. (The googles are important so no one gets shaving cream or cheese puffs in their eyes.) The team that gets the most cheese puffs stuck to the shaving cream (and their teammate's face) is the winner. There is usually always at least one good sport willing to put the shaving cream on and have cheese puffs tossed at them. While this game is messier and requires more clean-up time, it's a game that staff always have fun playing.

Count It Out: This game requires small, individual candies (e.g., Skittles or M&Ms), straws, and bowls. Each team chooses one teammate to stand on a designated spot with a bowl. The rest of the team stands a certain distance away with a straw. Nearby is another bowl (or a teammate holding another bowl). When the timer starts, teammates will use the straw to pick up a piece of candy from the bowl (with one hand behind their back). To pick up the candy, they have to suck through the straw to attach it. They then have to carry it over to and drop it in the second bowl. The team that transfers the most candy at the end of one minute is the winner.

Paper Toss: This game needs crumpled-up paper balls, clipboards or a sturdy book, and a basket or empty trash can. Each team starts several feet away from the basket. Partners use clipboards as paddles to hit the crumpled-up paper ball back and forth to each other until they get near the basket. The team that gets the most paper balls into the basket at the end of one minute is the winner.

Costume Contests

Costume contests are a great way to turn a normal day into something fun. There are obvious times of year when this could naturally occur, but since not everyone celebrates Halloween, you could reframe the day as Character Day. Think of ways you can make this even more engaging for staff. One idea is to have a team contest so it encourages groups of teachers to work together and dress as a theme. To add some extra fun, have a staff parade through the hallways or gymnasium so everyone can see and react to their costumes. Once a winner is named after the first year, that team can choose the winning team the following year.

Another dress-up day could be around winter break when you have a nondenominational ugly sweater contest. We typically make the entire last week before winter break a dress-up week because it promotes fun when so many are ready for a break. Some other ideas include specific costume prompts during spirit week and a "dress-down" day to break the monotony of the school year (especially if your school requires uniforms).

Organic Fun

The more organically fun is embedded into the workday, the more effective it will be (Everett, 2011). Costume contests that complement holidays and weekly events can feel organic with events already happening at work. The following are examples of other ways we prioritize fun without it becoming a chore or feeling forced.

If you already have a system in place for morning announcements, celebrating student growth goals (such as MAP scores, sight word recognition, and common formative assessment results) is a great way to incorporate organic fun. It could be a signal to have staff stop and dance to celebrate their students or to sing the school fight song. There are so many opportunities to embed fun into something as simple as this.

Another way to encourage fun without making it mandatory is to create a scavenger hunt that breaks up the monotony of the week. Staff might initially be reluctant to participate in something like this, but offering a random prize (e.g., a small gift card or free lunch) is usually enticing enough to encourage participation. An added benefit of this is that it should encourage staff to participate who might not otherwise. Think about a time you were encouraged to participate in an activity at a professional development session that you really had no desire to do, but once you got into the activity, you realized you needed the movement or the fun. Staff members respond in the same way. Though they may have only participated for the prize, they will reap the benefits of having fun along the way.

As you have likely realized by now, having fun with your staff can be important for a variety of reasons: building relationships, breaking up monotony, improving focus after a long day, and so much more. The most important part of promoting fun with staff is that it is used intentionally. When you incorporate fun for the right reasons, there will almost always be a great return for the amount of time you spent on the activity. Don't just take our word for it. Give it a try and watch how it transforms the energy in your building!

Think-Abouts

1. What do you already have in place that creates fun for your staff?

2. How could you embed fun into activities you already have planned to increase staff engagement?

3. If you already incorporate fun into the workplace, is it forced or organic in nature? In what ways can you ensure a balance so staff can release their stress through fun?

4. How much time are you willing to spend on fun to increase engagement and community? If you are short on time, how can you weave in some of these activities to make fun a priority?

5. In what ways are you modeling fun and not taking yourself too seriously?

9

Daily Sustainability

*"Nourishing yourself in a way that helps you blossom in the
direction you want to go is attainable, and you are worth the effort."*

—Deborah Day

🔋 Burnout Challenge

The need for increased social and emotional support has forced teachers to spend extra time filling in the gap of mental health shortages.
As teachers try to balance all the challenges associated with meeting
students' academic and social-emotional needs, they often ignore the
signs of secondary trauma. When this happens, compassion fatigue
sets in, which can lead to mental and physical exhaustion.

Mrs. Cortez stood at the front of her classroom, passionately teaching her
students about landforms and erosion. Her dedication to education was
unwavering, but she couldn't help but notice the toll it was taking on her
own well-being. Long hours, endless paperwork, and the weight of responsibility were all wearing her down.

One evening, as Mrs. Cortez sat at her desk, an administrator walked
past her classroom door. Surprised that she was still there, Dr. Thompson
popped her head in and asked if everything was OK. Recognizing that Mrs.

Cortez was, in fact, *not* OK, Dr. Thompson suggested that she practice self-care to restore her energy.

After Dr. Thompson left, Mrs. Cortez sunk into her chair even more as she thought, "Self-care? Is she serious right now? Is self-care the answer to everything? I am so sick of hearing those words! I am missing my daughter's soccer game right now, and she's telling me to practice self-care? As if I have time for that!"

The hard truth is that the need for increased social and emotional support has forced teachers to spend extra time filling the gap left by mental health shortages. As teachers try to balance all the challenges associated with meeting students' academic and social-emotional needs, they often ignore the signs of secondary trauma. When this happens, compassion fatigue can lead to mental and physical exhaustion.

In addition to appreciation and fun in the workplace, the next component that is critically important for reducing staff burnout is daily sustainability. Everyone in a school should focus on supporting the emotional well-being of students, but leaders also need to understand that supporting the emotional well-being of staff is a prerequisite.

Although self-care is critically important, it is such an overused term that most people tune out as soon as they hear the words. In addition, "quick fix" recommendations for self-care, such as taking a bath, lighting a candle, or taking a few minutes to meditate, minimize the emotional drainage we experience and imply that one activity will magically make all the stress disappear. For that reason, we've shifted our focus to strategies that can be used daily to create a model of sustainability, which can only be done through consistency. We call this daily sustainability.

The education profession can be emotionally taxing—not just because of the workload but because of all the ancillary factors relevant to teaching, not least of which is secondary trauma. Secondary trauma results from knowledge of a traumatizing event another person has experienced and shared with you (Motta, 2008). When students who experience trauma feel safe enough to talk with their teacher or other educational staff and share their experiences, it can create secondary trauma for that educator. Listening to these experiences, experiencing the situation vicariously, and then making a plan to keep students safe is a form of emotional labor that leads to emotional exhaustion (Keller et al., 2014).

This is just one of many factors relevant to today's teaching experience that result in more burnout. However, teacher burnout is not a new issue. Researchers have been studying the impact of burnout for decades, focused on the following areas, among others: burnout and teaching efficacy (Flook et al., 2013), reduction of teacher stress (Roeser et al. 2013), and the relationship between teacher burnout and student outcomes (Jennings & Greenberg, 2009).

The strategies throughout this chapter are designed to help decrease stress and refocus for the task at hand. Although this book offers ways to take instructional items off teachers' plates, this chapter focuses on strategies to help them melt away the stress and secondary trauma absorbed throughout the day. Each of the following components can be administered in as few as two minutes and gives instructions to model and/or lead employees through the calming activity.

Mindfulness

Mindfulness and meditation, though very similar, have a few distinct differences. Mindfulness is defined as being present without judgment (Kabat-Zinn, 2003). Therefore, it can be achieved in a variety of ways, such as a mindful walk, mindful eating, mindful movement, and more.

Think about the last time you had a meal. Were you present and aware of every bite you took? Or did your mind wander the entire time you were eating? Have you gotten home at the end of the day and realized you don't remember exactly how you got there? So much of our lives as adults is spent in our heads. We replay conversations we had with someone earlier in the day, hold conversations with someone that never happened, and get caught in those loops inside our head. This happens so frequently that it is easy to get stuck on autopilot.

Mindfulness shifts our awareness back to the present. That shift allows us to experience all the sensory input in that moment: what we hear, see, smell, touch, and maybe even taste. Being in the present and experiencing all our senses allows us to escape the loop that is playing on repeat in our head.

The benefits of mindfulness are many; most notably, research supports increased emotion regulation, self-esteem, empathy, and attention (Milligan et al., 2013). Best of all, mindfulness is a practice that should not take any additional time out of the day. It can be woven into and practiced during small moments that are already taking place. The only difference is your shift in attention to the present.

A focus on mindfulness in the classroom has been on the rise since 2016. Multiple studies (O'Conner et al., 2017; Schonert et al., 2015; Viglas & Perlman, 2018) have shown how it can be implemented in the classroom to have a positive effect on students, but one of the outcomes not typically discussed is the residual impact mindfulness can have on staff. Educators who are participating in and leading these activities will also see similar positive impacts. How amazing is that?

This chapter includes mindfulness strategies all staff can use to achieve sustainability and that have a profound impact on overall mental and emotional well-being. Most important, this chapter outlines ways administrators can not only support their own emotional well-being but also embed it into their school's culture to support staff. Due to the limited time that most teaching professionals have, these strategies are all designed to be completed in just one to two minutes, with an option to extend any of them based on personal needs and preferences.

Intention Setting

Setting a daily intention is a great way to start each day. In order to embed this into our school culture, we start morning announcements by asking students and staff to stop, find their anchor, and set an intention for whatever they want to bring into their day. This is a great way to help build mindfulness into the daily routine. Although setting an intention is important, it is really important to discuss and model the behaviors associated with this. There's often a gap between our ability to set an intention and the actual behavior that follows that intention. In short, there's more merit in setting an intention when there's a plan for implementing your intention (Webb et al., 2012). Therefore, teaching students and staff how to use and implement their intention is crucial for success.

The following is a guide on how to implement an intention:

- Decide what you want to bring into your day today (e.g., peace, love, compassion toward self or others).
- Post your intention somewhere you will see it. Hang it near your desk. Set it as a reminder or an alarm on your phone. Remind yourself often.
- When you feel yourself showing up in a way that is misaligned with your intention, pause, repeat your intention, and then react or respond appropriately.

Intentional Breathing

Focusing on our breathing is a simple way to regroup and recenter when we feel out of alignment or stressed during the day. Although it is a simple action, it is often something we forget about. Practicing different breathing patterns can help you get an idea of what works or feels best for you.

Box Breathing: This is a pattern of breathing that includes the same number of breaths (typically three or four) in the pattern of a square (Figure 9.1): breathe in, hold, breathe out, hold, repeat. To begin, place your finger at the bottom left corner. Trace the line of the square up as you breathe in. Continuing in a clockwise motion, trace your finger to the right and hold. As you trace your finger down, breathe out as steadily as you breathe in. Finally, trace the square to the left as you hold at the bottom. This can feel awkward because it is not our typical breathing pattern to hold at the bottom of the breath. However, that specific part of the box breath forces you to be present and can help you reset. Repeat this box breath pattern at least three times. If you are unable to physically trace the square, it is helpful to envision the square in your mind as you breathe.

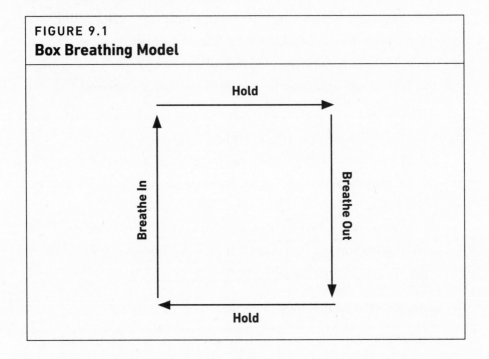

FIGURE 9.1
Box Breathing Model

This is a great strategy to use strategically at staff meetings. One purpose would be to simply introduce the box breath as a quick strategy to reduce and manage stress. To practice, hand out small squares so everyone has an opportunity for the tactile experience of tracing the square for their first time completing the strategy. Another use is to incorporate it throughout a meeting in which there is heavier content. When you feel that your staff needs a minute, pause and lead them through the box breath to reset before taking in additional information.

Paced Breathing: This particular breathing strategy activates mechanisms in the heart and respiratory system that reduce stress (University of California–Berkeley, 2024). However, it is important to start slow. If this is a new breathing strategy for you, the point of the breath is to have a longer exhale than inhale. The longer exhale is what activates stress reduction. Start by inhaling to a count of two and then exhale to a count of four. If that feels good, work your way up. Practicing this strategy allows your body to practice decreasing stress regardless of your stress level in the moment. It is important to practice this strategy so it becomes second nature, and remember to use it when your stress levels start to spike.

Again, this is a great strategy to use and model during staff meetings. Being that it is an easy strategy to incorporate throughout the day, this would be a great breathing pattern to practice and share with staff on one of the first days of the school year. Then embed it in staff meetings through-out the year to build muscle memory and help staff destress when they need it the most.

Guided Visualizations

Guided visualizations are a quick way to destress and bring your energy back to center. This practice can be done in any space where you feel safe. One of our favorite ways to practice a guided meditation is to find a comfortable seated position and close your eyes. Picture the most relaxing place you have ever been. Once you have a really clear vision of it in your mind, start noticing each of your five senses, one at a time. What do you see in that relaxing image? What things are around you? Is there anything you can hear while being in that space? If you were to put your hands down, is there anything you feel? Are there any scents in the air? Maybe you can even taste it. Spend a minute or two soaking in that space with as many senses as possible. When your time is up, gently bring yourself back to the present by wiggling your fingers and toes and then blinking open your eyes.

Many educators have limited time to themselves during the workday, so this practice may be best to do during the morning before work begins. It could also be done after work, in your car, before the routine of the rest of your day begins. If there is a morning that is particularly stressful as students and staff enter the building, this is an effective strategy to use in the morning announcements so everyone in the building has a chance to let go of any chaos or stress they brought into the building and prepare for a productive day. We find guided visualizations particularly helpful after a stressful day before you interact with your family. (It eliminates the consequence of projecting whatever happened during the day onto your loved ones.) Therefore, this could be used at the end of a staff meeting to help employees transition home to their families.

Habit Formation

A critical component of daily sustainability is using emotional regulation strategies routinely and regularly. You need to make it a habit. As you know, teaching is emotionally taxing because of the secondary trauma staff endures in addition to their normal daily responsibilities. When we go through periods of increased stress, most people tend to spend more time in a negative mental loop. When this happens, we also tend to resort to older habits because they don't require more thinking. In short, they're familiar and easy.

However, creating habits that support emotional regulation makes the process easier to sustain during times of heightened stress. When the habits are already formed, they don't require as much mental fortitude. This means the most effective way to deal with stress is to build meaningful habits. This could be done in the middle of a stressful time, but it could also be done during periods of less stress, such as summer or winter break. It may seem counterintuitive to start implementing stress-reducing strategies when you're not actually feeling much stress, but it actually provides an opportunity to build a strong habit with more mental acuity.

How do we build meaningful habits? Many people assume it requires an incredible amount of motivation. The truth is that motivation alone will not build habits. We need to be intentional. To that end, small changes, when combined, can make a huge impact (Clear, 2018). These "microhabits" add up over time and are incredibly efficient at making change. We also need to track the habits, using a specially designed habit tracking app, a paper checklist, or an accountability partner or coach.

Start with the basic habit tracker in Figure 9.2. Write your strategies in the first column, and check off each day that you practice the strategy. When building a habit, it's important to remember, especially at the beginning, that change can be difficult—especially when you're trying to add something new to your routine. If you forget, set a phone reminder, or post notes in conspicuous places around your home and workspace. Once it becomes more of a habit, it will get easier to do.

FIGURE 9.2 **Habit Tracker**							
Habit	**Sun**	**Mon**	**Tue**	**Wed**	**Thu**	**Fri**	**Sat**

Intentionality with Staff

In our district, the topic of self-care became a popular talking point during a time of high teacher stress. Teachers were feeling the burden of top-down decision making, so we decided to start lifting them up once a week through positive quotes and a light breakfast in the middle of the week when we all needed a boost. We called this Wellness Wednesday. It was such a hit, we still have Wellness Wednesdays now, many years later! Every week, we send out a slide deck with an inspirational story (which gives us an opportunity to get vulnerable and share personal stories with staff), a self-care strategy, a spotlight of the week for staff positivity, and motivational quotes. In addition, we also host a light breakfast for staff. This can be something as simple as some fruit and breakfast bars, or it can be more substantial with donuts, bacon, and coffee. A little bit goes a long way here.

Another way we promote self-care is through various challenges in which staff can earn rewards for participating. One example is a self-care bingo board. This can be built by choosing meaningful activities to add to the board (such as some of the strategies mentioned earlier). We avoided things such as "take a bath" or "light a candle" because most people are sick of hearing those two activities. Once the board was completed, staff were given a printed and electronic copy to choose how they wanted to indicate which bingo squares they completed. On the day of the deadline, staff turned in their hard copy or sent a screenshot of the electronic copy to enter to win a prize! For this activity specifically, we made it a point to ask local businesses for donations, and they delivered! When there are bigger prizes (like gift cards for a manicure or sauna appointment), there is greater buy-in from staff.

In addition to promoting self-care, it is imperative to model it. For us, that looked like sharing personal stories of self-care, posting self-care experiences to social media, and even taking a minute in the middle of the day to regroup before rushing to the next meeting. Discussing self-care is meaningful, but there is a much greater impact when your staff actually sees you practicing what you encourage them to do. Nevertheless, with the overuse of the term, we must be creative in how we talk about self-care with our staff and one another. Most important, don't just talk about it. Model self-care to demonstrate its importance in protecting your mental health. Self-care is a key component in mitigating teacher burnout!

While the ideas mentioned in this chapter might not be new for you, hopefully, the idea of consistently practicing the strategies and tracking your habit formation will be a game changer for you and your staff. When it becomes embedded in your school's culture through small intentional ways, it becomes much easier to model and promote. In the end, creating emotional and mental sustainability is imperative to retain high-quality staff.

Think-Abouts

1. How could you support these strategies for daily sustainability with your staff?
2. How could you include some of the strategies in this chapter without making them feel forced?
3. Which strategies could you incorporate into the student day that would have a secondary, vicarious impact on staff?
4. How important is it for you to support your staff's emotional well-being? How much time are you willing to dedicate to making sure that happens in an intentional way?

10

Combating Teacher and Substitute Shortages

"The future of the world is in my classroom today."

—Ivan Welton Fitzwater

> ## 🔋 Burnout Challenge
>
> Teacher shortages have always existed. However, there's been a steady decrease in the number of students pursuing education, and the negative narrative surrounding education on social media has prompted more teachers to leave the profession. School leaders nationwide are plagued with vacant classrooms and an empty candidate pool.

Principal McAllister sat at her desk, her brow furrowed with concern. The persistent challenge of teacher shortages weighed heavily on her shoulders, leaving her feeling frustrated and overwhelmed. The school year was about to begin, and the prospect of filling vacant positions seemed increasingly daunting.

As she contemplated the impact of teacher shortages, she couldn't help but reflect on the toll it took on her staff and students. Overworked teachers struggled to meet the demands of their classrooms, and students yearned for the stability and consistency that a full teaching roster could provide.

Teacher and substitute shortages make the work of a school much more difficult because of one obvious reason: students cannot be left alone to fend for themselves. Unfortunately, shortages are rampant across the United States (Walker, 2021). This book was written with burnout in mind to support your current staff and retain high-quality teachers. The current reality suggests that those efforts are crucial. Invariably, most schools have a handful of staff who are reliable and serve as the "go to" for almost any need. Yes, that is nice to have, but the current staffing shortage means it is impractical—if not impossible—to have the same staff take on extra responsibilities and add anything else to their plate. Not only will that burn out some of the best staff you have, but it will crumble the culture and climate you have worked so hard to build. This chapter, then, is designed to help you combat teacher shortages in meaningful and intentional ways without burning out your best teachers.

What are the related issues that teacher shortages create? Primarily, they leave classrooms in the hands of another employee (who may already have their own class) or a long-term substitute (if you are lucky). Typically, when a long-term substitute is assigned to a classroom, that person is not required to plan lessons, differentiate instruction, or take on any of the standard responsibilities of a classroom teacher. They're simply responsible for monitoring the class and delivering the lesson planned by someone else.

Some of this can be mitigated if your building already has collaborative planning. In an elementary or middle school, you likely have other teachers teaching the same content and planning similar lessons and assessments. Therefore, the gap in planning can be "easily" addressed. In high schools, though, it might be the case that only one person teaches a specific course. Therefore, your instructional coach may be essential in helping plan content. Another option is to partner with other local schools that may be willing to collaborate for needs specifically like this. If the relationship is reciprocal and not one-sided, both schools could benefit in the long term.

As common as teacher shortages are, schools are in the same predicament with many other positions: cafeteria workers, bus drivers, and substitutes, to name a few (Walker, 2021). A lack of substitutes creates an even bigger issue. When there are no substitutes to cover a classroom, then what? This is when you need to get creative to ensure that classrooms are covered and that you are supporting all staff who will inevitably have to help fill in. How is this done without destroying culture?

Get Staff Input

When you have vacancies, teachers are asked—sometimes mandated—to work through their planning periods to ensure other classes have appropriate coverage. In addition to further igniting teacher burnout, these additional requirements threaten the efficacy of your collaborative master schedule.

We've found that one of the best ways to lessen the stress of substitute shortages is to proactively create a plan and clearly communicate that plan with staff. Whenever possible, use non-classroom teachers (e.g., English language development teachers, instructional coaches, athletic directors). The plan we've implemented has two options:

- **Option 1:** Schedule staff in two-hour increments at various times for selected grade/subject levels. *Pro:* This allows teachers to have a small range of grades/subjects for which they are responsible, and it still leaves them with time in their day to conduct their "regular duties." *Con:* If the grade/subject has frequent absences, those teachers may have to sub more than others (who are assigned to another grade or subject), thus creating an inequitable distribution of responsibilities.
- **Option 2:** Schedule staff for full days of subbing assignments, based on where the vacancies exist. *Pro:* This allows a more equitable

distribution of responsibilities since they are spread out on a rotational basis. *Con:* There is less familiarity with the content because assignments can be in any grade or subject.

One of the most important proactive measures you can take as you create an effective plan is to meet with and get buy-in from all staff who will likely be affected and have to cover classrooms. When you meet, everyone should feel free to share their thoughts and give input on how they would be affected. Giving staff voice and choice will help solidify buy-in. Even if they may not be terribly excited about subbing, they at least have an opportunity to weigh in about a decision that will seriously affect (i.e., disrupt) their day.

Give Advanced Notice

It's imperative to give staff who need to cover a class as much notice as possible. Showing up to work for the day and then finding out you have to completely pivot your plans for the day does not feel good for anyone. Sometimes that is unavoidable, but if there is any possibility that someone will have to sub, they should be aware. This allows them to mentally prepare and shift around their other daily tasks. If a sub does show up and they no longer have to provide coverage, that is a much better surprise than the reverse!

When you ask staff to do something outside of their typical scope of responsibility, it is crucial to find things you can take off their plate. Instead of just giving them more to do, you need to help minimize or outsource some of the other tasks for which they are responsible. Staff are more willing to be flexible when they know that this isn't just one more thing—especially if this happens frequently. Consider utilizing community and family partnerships to help with tedious tasks (e.g., cleaning lunch tables between classes, organizing books in the library) so staff can shift around as needed.

Foster Relationships with Substitutes

One way to foster relationships is by changing the language we use. There can be a negative connotation with the term *substitute*. In Chapter 7, we mentioned that we often refer to substitutes as guest teachers. Some may consider this just semantics, but a subtle shift in terms can have a much larger impact. (For consistency and familiarity purposes, we will continue to use the term *substitute* here.) When substitutes show up in your building, go out of your way to make them feel welcome and like they belong. Building relationships with substitutes and making them feel like they are part of the school community is a great way to make someone want to come back when the opportunity arises.

Not sure how to do this? Here are some things that you can try. If you are planning something for staff appreciation (or any other staff event throughout the day), include the substitutes who are in the building. Appreciation works for everyone, not just your permanent staff. Try having a gift bag ready for the subs who work in your school. It could be something as simple as a bag of chips and a bottle of water to give them a boost as they walk in the door. If you don't have the funds for this, simply go out of your way to greet and welcome subs. When an administrator and other school staff are kind and welcoming, it makes people want to be there.

Many times, you can set a positive tone for your relationship with substitutes before they even step foot in the building. We've found that adding a personal connection, by calling or texting possible subs to introduce yourself and ask about their availability, garners an increased rate of acceptances over just using the school's substitute system. A contact list for preferred subs is also beneficial to distribute. This ensures the information is readily available when a teacher needs to be absent.

If you really want substitutes to come back, have systems and structures in place to help support them. For example, in addition to lesson plans and other important documents, think about including a standard template to share important information about classroom management (such as signals all students use), how to get administrator support if needed, and which students have severe allergies in the substitute folder to help increase the likelihood of success and job satisfaction (see Figure 10.1). Having a standard template ensures all necessary information is shared in an easily read document, and, if you have recurring subs, they already know what to expect and where to find it. This helps set them up for success!

Finally, if a substitute is working in a classroom where there are known behavioral issues, have a plan to support them. Perhaps a buddy teacher checks in frequently to provide the substitute or specific students with a necessary break. Maybe a behavior coach visits the classroom a few extra times on that particular day. The instructional coach could even go into the classroom to provide part of a lesson, which also lets them check on the behaviors.

Plan for Late Arrivals and Early Dismissals

Most doctors, therapists, and other medical/mental health support tend to work the same hours as educators. Therefore, most appointments will likely take people away from the workday. As administrators, you hold the power to decide whether you will allow staff to have a late arrival or an early dismissal. There are definitely things to consider when someone requests time off, but is it worth having a teacher out for an entire day when they may only need to miss an hour of work?

Finding coverage for a short amount of time is usually much easier than finding coverage for an entire day. Considerations for arriving late or leaving early are entirely up to you and your staff. However, common considerations include the time they will miss from the day and how often the request is made.

Having a strategic proactive plan for times when there is no substitute to cover a classroom not only cuts down on last-minute scrambling but also allows staff to schedule their own time and figure out how best to shift their other responsibilities. Though painful, teacher and substitute shortages

FIGURE 10.1
Sample Classroom Management Plan

Classroom Management Plan	
Teacher	**Room #**

Walkie-Talkie Codes for Support	
Code 1	One additional administrator or behavior support team member needed to respond to help a student in their classroom
Code 3	All student response team members needed to support an emergency situation (e.g., a fight, medical emergency, or student throwing things across the room)

Class Attention Signal

Opening Procedures	
Entering the room	
Morning work	
Arriving late	
Getting materials	
Other	

Work-Time Expectations	
Turning in work	
Independent work	
Group work	
Transitions	
Getting assistance	
Other	

Response to Behavior	
TAB in location in classroom	
TAB out location outside classroom	
Parent communication	
Student helpers	
Special student considerations	
Restroom	
Partner teacher (if questions)	

Closing Procedures	
Cleaning up	
Dismissal	

Medication	
Students	Time (send to main office)

Student Allergies	
Students	Allergies

can be handled in a way that lessens the impact on staff. And when handled effectively, it reduces the chances of further burning out your staff, making all of this effort worth it.

While all these chapters hold the possibility of making meaningful change in reducing the burnout of your staff, implementing them all together is where the magic happens. When you reach that point, that is when teacher burnout becomes so minimal that it eliminates concerns of teacher retention and elevates the instructional impact on students.

Think-Abouts

1. What proactive plan can you put into place for teacher and substitute shortages?
2. How can you foster relationships with the substitutes who show up to your building so they want to come back?
3. When another teacher has to cover a classroom, what are some creative ways you can take responsibilities off their plate to help out?
4. What systems do you already have in place that could be tweaked to streamline the process for substitutes in your building?

References

Aguilar, E. (2020). *Coaching for equity: Conversations that change practice.* Jossey-Bass.

Ali, B. J., Anwar, G., Gardi, B., Othman, B. J., Aziz, H. M., Ahmed, S. H., Hamza, P. A., Ismael, N. B., Sorguli, S., & Sabir, B. Y. (2021). Business communication strategies: Analysis of internal communication processes. *Journal of Humanities and Education Development, 3*(3), 16–38.

Babin Dhas, D., & Karthikeyan, P. (2015). Work-life balance challenges and solutions: Overview. *International Journal of Research in Humanities and Social Studies, 12*(2), 10–19.

Betz, A. (2023). Teacher burnout: Warning signs, causes and tips on how to avoid. www.educationcorner.com/teacher-burnout.html

Bodenheimer, G. (2018). Emotional labour, teaching and burnout: Investigating complex relationships. *Educational Research, 62*(1), 63–76.

BrightHR. (2016). Wellbeing in the workplace: Putting cloud9 to work. www.brighthr.com/blog/healthy-minds/wellbeing-in-the-workplace-putting-cloud9-to-work

Brown, B. (2018). *Dare to lead.* Random House.

Bryant, J., Ram, S., Scott, D., & Williams, C. (2023). K–12 teachers are quitting. What would make them stay? www.mckinsey.com/industries/education/our-insights/k-12-teachers-are-quitting-what-would-make-them-stay

Bryk, A. S., & Schneider, B. (2002). *Trust in schools.* Russell Sage Foundation.

Campbell, J., & van Nieuwerburgh, C. (2018). *The leader's guide to coaching in schools: Creating conditions for effective learning.* Corwin.

Center on PBIS. (2022). Positive behavioral interventions and supports. www.pbis.org

Chapman, G., & White, P. (2019). *The 5 languages of appreciation in the workplace: Empowering organizations by encouraging people.* Moody.

Chazin, K. T., Velez, M. S., & Ledford, J. R. (2021). Reducing escape without escape extinction: A systematic and meta-analysis of escape-based interventions. *Journal of Behavioral Education, 31*, 186–215.

Clear, J. (2018). *Atomic habits: An easy & proven way to build good habits & break bad ones.* Avery.

Cornett, J., & Knight, J. (2009). Research on coaching. In J. Knight (Ed.), *Coaching: Approaches and perspectives* (pp. 192–216). Corwin.

Darbishire, P., Isaacs, A. N., & Miller, M. L. (2020). Faculty burnout in pharmacy education. *American Journal of Pharmaceutical Education, 84*(7), ajpe7925.

Doran, G. T. (1981). There's a S.M.A.R.T. way to write management's goals and objectives. *Management Review, 70*, 35–36.

DuFour, R., DuFour, R., Eaker, R., & Many, T. (2010). *Learning by doing* (2nd ed.). Solution Tree.

Everett, A. (2011). Benefits and challenges of fun in the workplace. *Library Leadership & Management*, 1–25.

Flook, L., Goldberg, S. B., Pinger, L., Bonus, K., & Davidson, R. J. (2013). Mindfulness for teachers: A pilot study to assess effects on stress, burnout, and teaching efficacy. *Mind, Brain, & Education, 7*, 182–195.

Garcia, E., & Weiss, E. (2019). Challenging working environments ('school climates'), especially in high-poverty schools, play a role in the teacher shortage. www.epi.org/publication/school-climate-challenges-affect-teachers-morale-more-so-in-high-poverty-schools-the-fourth-report-in-the-perfect-storm-in-the-teacher-labor-market-series

Gomez, D. (n.d.). Why teachers quit + top signs quitting teaching is the right move. https://teachercareercoach.com/why-teachers-quit

Grissom, J. A., Loeb, S., & Master, B. (2013). Effective instructional time use for school leaders: Longitudinal evidence from observations of principals. *Educational Researcher, 42*(8), 433–444.

Handley, J. (Host). (2022, September 9). Creating a culture that supports the big people so they can support the little people (S7 E11) [Audio podcast episode]. In *Be the Leader You Deserve*. https://podcasts.apple.com/us/podcast/s7-e11-creating-a-culture-that-supports-the-big/id1522933343?i=1000578937346

Hattie, J. (2019). *Visible learning for teachers: Maximizing impact on learning*. Routledge.

Hord, S. M. (1997). *Professional learning communities: Communities of continuous inquiry and improvement*. Southwest Education Development Laboratory.

Jennings, P. A., & Greenberg, M. T. (2009). The prosocial classroom: Teacher social and emotional competence in relation to student and classroom outcomes. *Review of Educational Research, 79*, 491–525.

Kabat-Zinn, J. (2003). Mindfulness-based stress reduction (MBSR). *Constructivism in the Human Sciences, 8*(2), 73–107.

Keller, M. M., Chang, M. L., Becker, E. S., Goetz, T., & Frenzel, A. C. (2014). Teachers' emotional experiences and exhaustion as predictors of emotional labor in the classroom: An experience sampling study. *Frontiers in Psychology, 5*, 1–10.

Kentucky Department of Education. (2022). Educator development and equity: A4 modules. www.education.ky.gov/teachers/Pages/A4-Modules.aspx

Laird, M., & Cain, S. (2011). *The fundamental 5: The formula for quality instruction*. CreateSpace.

Lane, K. L., & Menzies, H. M. (2009). Student risk screening scale for early internalizing and externalizing behavior (SRSS-IE). www.ci3t.org/screening#srssie

Larson, K. E., Pas, E. T., Bradshaw, C. P., Rosenberg, M. S., & Day-Vines, N. L. (2018). Examining how proactive management and culturally responsive teaching relate to student behavior: Implications for measurement and practice. *School Psychology Review, 47*(2), 153–166.

Long, J. (2010). The fatal attraction of mentoring: Mentoring for retention of beginning teachers. *International Journal of Interdisciplinary Social Sciences, 5*(2), 265–274.

Luhombo, K. K., Omondi, D. O., & Aswani, D. R. (2023). Effective internal communication and teacher burnout: A review of relevant literature. *Kabarak Journal of Research & Innovation, 13*(2), 38–47.

Martinez, L. A. M., & Hurtado, S. R. F. (2018). Internal communication issues in firms: Does it affect the productivity? *Review of European Studies 10*(2), 1–13.

Marzano, R., Waters, T., & McNulty, B. (2005). *School leadership that works: From research to results.* ASCD.

Maslach, C., & Leither, M. P. (2016). Understanding the burnout experience: Recent research and its implications for psychiatry. *World Psychiatry, 15*(2), 103–111.

Milligan, K., Badali, P., & Spiroiu, F. (2013). Using integrated mindfulness martial arts to address self-regulation challenges in youth with learning disabilities: A qualitative exploration. *Journal of Child and Family Studies, 24,* 562–575.

Mitchell, B. S., Kern, L., & Conroy, M. A. (2018). Supporting students with emotional or behavioral disorders: State of the field. *Behavioral Disorders, 44*(2), 70–84.

Molero, P., Zurita Ortega, F., Ubago Jimenez, J., & Gonzalez Valero, G. (2019). Influence of emotional intelligence and burnout syndrome on teacher well-being: A systematic review. *Social Sciences, 8*(6), 185.

Motta, R. W. (2008). Secondary trauma. *International Journal of Emergency Mental Health, 10*(4), 291–298.

Newton, R. (2015). What kind of leader do you want to be? *Harvard Business Review.* https://hbr.org/2015/01/what-kind-of-leader-do-you-want-to-be

Oberg, G., Carroll, A., & Macmahon, S. (2023). Compassion fatigue and secondary traumatic stress in teachers: How they contribute to burnout and how they are related to trauma-awareness. www.frontiersin.org/articles/10.3389/feduc.2023.1128618/full

O'Conner, R., De Feyter, J., Carr, A., Luo, J. L., Romm, H., Regional Educational Laboratory Mid-Atlantic (ED), & ICF International. (2017). A review of the literature on social and emotional learning for students ages 3–8: Outcomes for different student populations and settings (Part 4 of 4). REL 2017-248. Regional Educational Laboratory Mid-Atlantic. http://search.ebscohost.com.libsrv.wku.edu/login.aspx?direct=true&db=eric&AN=ED572724&site=ehost-live

Pemberton, S. (2021). *The lighthouse effect: How ordinary people can have an extraordinary impact in the world.* Zondervan.

Rankin, J. G. (2016). The teacher burnout epidemic, part 1 of 2. *Psychology Today.* www.psychologytoday.com/us/blog/much-more-common-core/201611/the-teacher-burnout-epidemic-part-1-2

Rankin, J. G. (2022). How COVID increased teacher burnout: Preventing burnout in the COVID era. *Psychology Today.* www.psychologytoday.com/us/blog/much-more-than-common-core/202210/how-covid-increased-teacher-burnout

Richardson, B. K., Alexander, A., & Castleberry, T. (2008). Examining teacher turn-over in low-performing, multi-cultural schools: Relationships among emotional labor, communication symmetry, and intent to leave. *Communication Research Reports, 25*(1), 10–22.

Roeser, R. W., Schonert-Reichl, K. A., Jha, A., Cullen, M., Wallace, L., Wilensky, R., Oberle, E., Thomson, K., Taylor, C., & Harrison, J. (2013). Mindfulness training and reductions in teacher stress and burnout: Results from two randomized, wait-list-control field trials. *Journal of Educational Psychology, 105*, 787–804.

Ryan, R., & Deci, E. (2000). Self-determination theory and the facilitation of intrinsic motivation, social development, and well-being. *American Psychologist, 55*(1), 68–78.

Sailor, W., Skrtic, T. M., Cohn, M., & Olmstead, C. (2021). Preparing teacher educators for statewide scale-up of multi-tiered system of support (MTSS). *Teacher Education and Special Education, 44*(1), 24–41.

Salamondra, T. (2021). Effective communication in schools. *BU Journal of Graduate Studies in Education, 13*(1), 22–25.

Schonert, K. A., Oberle, E., Lawlor, M. S., Abbott, D., Thomson, K., Oberlander, T. F., & Diamond, A. (2015). Enhancing cognitive and social-emotional development through a simple-to-administer mindfulness-based school program for elementary school children: A randomized controlled trial. *Developmental Psychology, 51*(1), 52–66.

Sinek, S. (2009). *Start with why: How great leaders inspire everyone to take action.* Portfolio Penguin.

Sinek, S., Mead., D., & Docker, P. (2017). *Find your why: A practical guide for discovering purpose for you and your team.* Portfolio Penguin.

Skrabanek, B. (2022). Difference between vision and mission statements: 25 examples. *ClearVoice.* www.clearvoice.com/blog/difference-between-mission-vision-statement-examples

Sparks, S. D. (2022). Pandemic anxiety was higher for teachers than for health-care workers. https://www.edweek.org/teaching-learning/pandemic-anxiety-was-higher-for-teachers-than-for-health-care-workers/2022/11

Teamann, A., & Miller, M. (2019). *Lead with appreciation: Fostering a culture of gratitude.* Dave Burgess Consulting.

Tyler, D. E. (2016). Communication behaviors of principals at high performing Title I elementary schools in Virginia: School leaders, communication, and transformative efforts. *Creighton Journal of Interdisciplinary Leadership, 2*(2), 2–16.

University of California, Berkeley. (2024). Breathing exercises. https://uhs.berkeley.edu/sites/default/files/breathing_exercises_0.pdf

van Nieuwerburgh, C. (2017). *An introduction to coaching skills: A practical guide* (2nd ed.). Sage.

Viglas, M., & Perlman, M. (2018). Effects of a mindfulness-based program on young children's self-regulation, prosocial behavior and hyperactivity. *Journal of Child and Family Studies, 27*, 1150–1161.

Walker, T. (2021). *Getting serious about teacher burnout.* www.nea.org/advocating-for-change/new-from-nea/getting-serious-about-teacher-burnout

Walker, T. (2022). *Survey: Alarming number of educators may soon leave the profession*. National Education Association. www.nea.org/nea-today/all-news-articles/survey-alarming-number-educators-may-soon-leave-profession

Webb, T. L., Schweiger Gallo, I., Miles, E., Gollwitzer, P. M., & Sheeran, P. (2012). Effective regulation of affect: An action control perspective on emotion regulation. *European Review of Social Psychology, 23*(1), 143–186.

Woolf, N. (n.d.). *Morning meetings: Cultivating a culture of care and safety*. Panorama Education.

Yao, X., Yao, M., Zong, X., Li, Y., Li, X., Guo, F., & Cui, G. (2015). How school climate influences teachers' emotional exhaustion: The mediating role of emotional labor. *International Journal of Environmental Research and Public Health, 12*, 12505–12517.

Yin, H. (2011). Adaptation and validation of the teacher emotional labour strategy scale in China. *Educational Psychology, 32*, 451–465.

Index

The letter *f* following a page locator denotes a figure.

About the Authors

**Jill Handley**, EdD, is the assistant superintendent of multilingual learners in Jefferson County Public Schools (Kentucky), the 30th largest urban school district in the nation. Prior to this role, she was the award-winning principal of Kenwood Elementary. During her 16-year tenure as principal, she led her school to be recognized for several achievements, including National School of Character, National Distinguished ESEA School, and the first Family Friendly Certified school in the state of Kentucky. Handley is a highly sought after speaker and presenter and inspires educators from around the world through her highly engaging workshop sessions. In addition to leading her own school, she mentors new and aspiring principals, has authored and been featured in a variety of publications, and is the host of Be The Leader You Deserve podcast. In 2017, Handley was named the Hilliard Lyons Principal of the Year. Despite all this recognition, she is most proud of the culture and climate she and Lara Donnelly created and cultivated to ensure their students' success and high levels of satisfaction and retention of their teachers. Handley is also the proud mom of two daughters, Sydney and Madison, and considers them both to be her greatest accomplishments.

**Lara Donnelly**, EdD, is a veteran teacher and school counselor In Jefferson County Public Schools (Kentucky). She is an education consultant, speaker, and author supporting schools and administrators with burnout, family engagement, and multilingual learners with trauma and mental health concerns. Donnelly was recognized as the JCPS Outstanding Elementary School Counselor of the Year in 2018 and has been featured in podcasts, news articles, and televised interviews for her expertise in supporting mental health. In addition, she has presented at numerous national conferences, including ASCD, ESEA, and the Whole School REACH conference. Donnelly resides in Louisville, Kentucky, and can often be found fueling her passion for life by spending time with her daughter, MK, and her dog, Bo, and by cycling on the best trails in the state.

Related ASCD Resources: Teacher Burnout

At the time of publication, the following resources were available (ASCD stock numbers in parentheses).

The Burnout Cure: Learning to Love Teaching Again by Chase Mielke (#119004)

The EQ Way: How Emotionally Intelligent School Leaders Navigate Turbulent Times by Ignacio Lopez (#123046)

Embracing MESSY Leadership: How the Experience of 20,000 School Leaders Can Transform You and Your School by Alyssa Gallagher and Rosie Connor (#124011)

Every Connection Matters: How to Build, Maintain, and Restore Relationships Inside the Classroom and Out by Michael Creekmore and Nita Creekmore (#123010)

Illuminate the Way: The School Leader's Guide to Addressing and Preventing Teacher Burnout by Chase Mielke (#123032)

Make Teaching Sustainable: Six Shifts That Teachers Want and Students Need by Paul Emerich France (#123011)

Overcoming Educator Burnout (Quick Reference Guide) by Chase Mielke (#QRG123016)

Rekindle Your Professional Fire: Powerful Habits for Becoming a More Well-Balanced Teacher by Mike Anderson (#124027)

School Culture Rewired: Toward a More Positive and Productive School for All, 2nd Edition by Steve Gruenert and Todd Whitaker (#123029)

For up-to-date information about ASCD resources, go to www.ascd.org. You can search the complete archives of *Educational Leadership* at www.ascd.org/el.

ASCD myTeachSource®

Download resources from a professional learning platform with hundreds of research-based best practices and tools for your classroom at http://myteach-source.ascd.org.

For more information, send an email to member@ascd.org; call 1-800-933-2723 or 703-578-9600; send a fax to 703-575-5400; or write to Information Services, ASCD, 2800 Shirlington Road, Suite 1001, Arlington, Virginia USA.